'The second novel to appear in English by the bestselling Japanese author Mieko Kawakami is tauter and even more perceptive than its predecessor . . . *Heaven* is less than half the length and holds double the emotional force'

New Statesman

'Taking two outcast teens as its unhappy protagonists, [*Heaven*] is an expertly told, deeply unsettling tale of adolescent violence that will, no doubt, only grow the author's fan base'

Vogue

'Kawakami never evangelizes, never wags a finger. She simply sets first-person narrations of suffering alongside stumbling dialogues, attempts to make that suffering intelligible to others . . . This is the real magic of *Heaven*, which shows us how to think about morality as an ongoing, dramatic activity. It can be maddening and ruinous and isolating. But it can also be shared, enlivened through writing and conversation, and momentarily redeemed through unheroic acts of solidarity, which come more naturally to the children in *Heaven* than to most grownups here on earth'

Merve Emre, *New Yorker*

'Reading *Heaven* is a rare, unforgettable experience. For me this is a perfect novel, and one I know I will return to before long'

Megan Nolan, author of *Acts of Desperation*

'Short but assured . . . by the end, the reader is so dizzily absorbed in its visceral details and philosophical complexity that, when the twist comes, it hits you with a strange and unexpected force'

Financial Times

HEAVEN

Mieko Kawakami is the author of the internationally bestselling novel *Breasts and Eggs*, a *New York Times* Notable Book of the Year and one of *TIME*'s Best 10 Books of 2020. Born in Osaka, Kawakami made her literary debut as a poet in 2006, and published her first novella, *My Ego, My Teeth, and the World*, in 2007. Her writing is known for its poetic qualities and its insights into the female body, ethical questions, and the dilemmas of modern society. Her works have been translated into many languages and are available all over the world. She has received numerous prestigious literary awards in Japan for her work, including the Akutagawa Prize, the Tanizaki Prize, and the Murasaki Shikibu Prize. She lives in Tokyo, Japan.

Also by Mieko Kawakami

Breasts and Eggs
All the Lovers in the Night

Mieko Kawakami

HEAVEN

*Translated from the Japanese
by Sam Bett and David Boyd*

PICADOR

First published 2021 by Europa Editions, New York

First published in the UK 2021 by Picador

This paperback edition first published 2022 by Picador
an imprint of Pan Macmillan
The Smithson, 6 Briset Street, London EC1M 5NR
EU representative: Macmillan Publishers Ireland Ltd, 1st Floor,
The Liffey Trust Centre, 117–126 Sheriff Street Upper,
Dublin 1, D01 YC43
Associated companies throughout the world
www.panmacmillan.com

ISBN 978-1-5098-9825-1

10

A CIP catalogue record for this book is available from the British Library.

Printed and bound by CPI Group (UK) Ltd, Croydon, CR0 4YY

Visit **www.picador.com** to read more about all our books
and to buy them. You will also find features, author interviews and
news of any author events, and you can sign up for e-newsletters
so that you're always first to hear about our new releases.

HEAVEN

CHAPTER ONE

One day toward the end of April, between classes, I unzipped my pencil case and found a folded triangle of paper between the pencils.

I unfolded it to see what was inside.

"We should be friends."

That's all it said. Thin letters that looked like little fish-bones, written in mechanical pencil.

I quickly folded it up and slid it back into my pencil case. Taking a breath, I paused a second before looking around the room as casually as possible. The same group of classmates joking around and howling, the usual break between classes. I tried to calm myself down by repeatedly straightening my textbooks and notebooks, then I sharpened a pencil, taking my time. Before long, the bell rang for third period. Chair legs screeched across the floor. The teacher walked into the room and class began.

The note had to be a prank, but I had no idea why those guys would try something so subtle after all this time. I sighed in my mind, settling into the usual darkness.

Only that first note was left inside my pencil case. After that, they were taped to the inside of my desk, clinging to the underside, where my hand would easily detect them. Whenever I found a note, I got goosebumps. I scanned the classroom, careful not to get caught, but it always felt like somebody noticed my reaction. I was overtaken by a strange anxiety, at a loss for how to act.

"What were you doing yesterday, when it was raining?"

"If you could go to any country in the world, where would you go?"

Pieces of paper the size of postcards with simple questions written on them. I always went to the bathroom to read them. I would've thrown them away, but unable to decide where, I ended up stuffing them behind the dark blue cover of my planner.

Nothing seemed different after the notes started.

Almost every day, Ninomiya and the others made me carry their backpacks, or kicked me like it was nothing, or whacked me on the head with their recorders, or made me run around for them. But the notes kept showing up, and the messages grew longer. They never used my name, and they were never signed, but when I took a good look at the handwriting, I started wondering if maybe it wasn't Ninomiya or any of those guys, but someone else entirely. But I knew it was a dumb idea, and all my other thoughts crowded that one out of my mind, leaving me feeling even worse.

All the same, checking each morning for a new note became my little ritual. I started coming in early, when there was no one in the classroom, and it was quiet, a faint smell of oil in the air. It made me feel good to read those little letters. I never lost sight of the possibility that this might be a trap, but something in those notes made me feel safe, however briefly, even with all my distress.

At the start of May, just before vacation, I got a note saying, "I want to see you. Meet me after school. I'll be there, from five to seven." There was a date and a simple, hand-drawn map. I could hear my heart throbbing in my ears. I read the note so many times that I could see the words before me, even when I closed my eyes. I spent the rest of the day wondering what to do and thought of nothing else during recess, to the point that my head started to hurt and I lost my appetite. There was no doubt in my mind that when I showed up at the spot, Ninomiya and the others would be there waiting, ready to deliver the beating of a lifetime. Seeing me show up, they'd circle around and revel in their latest game at my expense. Things were only going to get worse.

But I couldn't just forget it.

When the day came, there was nothing I could do to settle down. The whole day in class, I kept an eye on Ninomiya and his friends as best I could, but I couldn't detect any significant change in their behavior. Eventually one of them noticed and said, "Hey, what're you looking at?" and whipped one of his classroom slippers at me. It smacked me in the face then dropped to the floor. He told me to pick it up, so I did.

By the end of the day, I was so worked up that I was feeling queasy. As soon as last period was over, I ran almost all the way home. As I was running, I asked myself if I was really going, what the hell I was doing, but no matter how I thought it through I couldn't say for sure. I had the feeling that anything I chose to do would turn out wrong.

When my mom saw me come home, she said hi from the couch where she was sitting and then turned back to the TV. I said hi back. A voice on the TV was delivering the news. It was the only sound in the house. Every room was quiet, same as always.

"I've been in the kitchen all day," my mom said.

I grabbed the carton of grapefruit juice from the fridge, poured a glass, and drank it at the counter. My mom looked over and told me to drink it at the table. A few seconds later, I heard the sound of fingernails or maybe toenails being clipped.

"You mean making dinner?"

"Uh-huh. Can't you smell it? My first pot roast, tied up with string!"

I wondered if my dad was actually coming home for once, but decided not to ask.

"You want to eat soon?"

"No. I need to go to the library for a bit. Later is fine."

My town has a big tree-lined street that goes on for blocks and blocks.

This is the route I took to school. To get to the meeting place, you turned left exactly halfway down the street with the trees, onto a side street leading to a sandy lot that barely qualified as a park.

Since I had left the house at four, there was no one at the spot when I arrived. I took the chance to catch my breath. There was a kind of bench made from tires on their sides, and a concrete whale, and between them a sandbox not much bigger than a mattress, littered with candy wrappers and plastic bags.

Among the trash, I could make out all these dry clumps of dog or cat crap. The way the sand stuck to them, they almost looked like tempura. I tried to count the individual nuggets, but new ones kept popping up. The whole sandbox was probably full of them. Then it hit me. Whoever called me here might force me to eat them. The back of my throat burned. I emptied my lungs, in an attempt to make the taste of the crap go away, but the thought alone made me sick.

The mouth of the whale was big enough for two people my size to fit inside. The paint had worn away so much you couldn't tell what color it used to be. People had tagged its back and its head with permanent marker. The lot fell in the shadow of an old apartment complex, and the ground was almost black, like something rotting.

I had some time to kill, so I walked back to the tree-lined street. I sat down on a metal bench, let out a huge sigh and breathed in slowly. I kept thinking how I'd made a mistake coming here, but if I hadn't, and Ninomiya and the others didn't get their way, I'd pay for it in the end. I told myself it didn't really matter what I did. Nothing would change.

I sighed again and looked up, feeling a little dazed. Not long ago, the trees were just a bunch of black trunks, but now their leaves were showing, and when the wind blew you could hear them rustle. I took off my glasses and rubbed my eyes, then looked up the street again. As usual, the world was flat and lacking depth. My eyes took in the scenery like a postcard, but when I blinked, it slipped from view, replaced by a new scene.

A little while later, still basically unable to think, I returned to the spot. I saw someone sitting on the tires with her back to me. A girl in her school uniform. This was a surprise. I looked around the lot for somebody else, but there was no sign of anyone.

I approached her cautiously. When I stopped near the mouth of the whale, she heard my footsteps and turned to face me. It was Kojima. From class. She stood up and looked me over, dropping her chin slightly. I did the same.

"The letter?"

Kojima was short, with kind of dark skin. She never talked at school. Her shirt was always wrinkled, and her uniform looked old. She never stood up straight. She had tons of hair, and it was totally black. So thick it never fell flat. The ends shot out in every direction. She had this dark spot under her nose, like dirt or maybe hair, and she got made fun of for it. The girls in class picked on her for being poor and dirty.

"I didn't think you'd come," Kojima laughed, smiling uneasily. "Were you weirded out?"

I couldn't think of what to say, so I shook my head. For a minute both of us just stood there silently.

"Sit down," Kojima said. I nodded and tried, but I couldn't sit right on the tires.

"It's not like I have something to tell you. I just thought we should talk, the two of us. Honestly, I felt like we both needed it. I guess I've felt that way for a long time now."

Kojima stumbled every few words. I realized this was the first time I had heard her voice. The first time I had ever seen her face straight on. It was also the first time I had ever talked like this with a girl. My palms were moist. I was sweaty all over. I didn't know where it was safe to look.

"I'm glad you came."

Her voice wasn't high or low, but it was firm, like there was something at its center, holding it together. I kept on nodding. Kojima noticed and seemed reassured.

"You know the name of this park?"

I shook my head.

"Whale Park. See? The whale's right there. Well, I guess I'm the only one who calls it that." She laughed. I imagined myself saying it. Whale Park.

"Like I said, I've wanted to talk for a while. That's why I wrote you those letters. But I didn't think you'd really come. I'm kind of in shock right now." She was rubbing her nose and speaking faster than before.

I nodded at this.

"I want to be friends," she said, looking at me. "I mean, if you're okay with that."

I didn't understand what she was saying, but I agreed. I felt a surge of misgivings. What did it mean for us to be friends? What was a friend supposed to do? I couldn't bring myself to ask. Sweat dripped down my back. Kojima smiled. She looked really happy to hear my answer. She let out a breath and told me she was glad. Then she stood up from the tires and brushed off the back of her skirt with both hands. Her skirt had these huge creases crossing the lines of the pleats. The pockets of her blazer were bulging with what looked like scraps of tissue.

"Happamine." She sounded like she was sighing, but never

broke her smile as she looked down at her feet. In my head I was, like, happawhat? I wanted to ask her what she said, but I wasn't sure of when or how to ask. I wound up saying nothing.

"Can I write you another letter?"

"Yeah," I said. My voice cracked. My face was hot.

"And give it to you?"

"Yeah." I nodded.

"You'll write back?"

"Yeah," I said. This time I spoke at the right volume. What a relief.

We stood there for a while, not saying anything. I could hear crows cawing somewhere far away.

"Bye."

Kojima smiled and looked at me, then gave me a tiny wave, spun around and walked up the side street leading to the street of trees.

She didn't look back. Not even once. In my eyes, it looked like there were two of her, almost overlapping, getting smaller and smaller. I wasn't sure how long you were supposed to watch someone walk away, but I watched until I couldn't see her anymore. I could still see the square bottom of her skirt swing like something heavy, swatting the backs of her calves. Even after she had completely disappeared, the bulky action of her skirt stayed with me.

"Not so fast, Eyes."

Class was over, but I turned around, because I had no choice, as rotten as I felt. One of Ninomiya's friends grabbed me by the neck and dragged me back into the classroom. This happened all the time. Ninomiya was in the middle of the room, sitting on a desk. That was his style. When he noticed me, he laughed, then said, "Hey buddy." He told me to shove a stick of chalk up my nose and draw something hilarious on the blackboard with it, something that would make them shit their pants. His friends all cracked up. One of them dragged me to the blackboard and the rest of them circled around to watch.

I'd known Ninomiya since elementary school.

Even then, he was the center of attention. He was the best athlete in our grade, but he also got straight A's, and he had a chiseled face that anybody would consider beautiful. We were all supposed to wear a navy sweater, but he wore whatever color he wanted. His hair came down to his shoulders. His older brother, three years ahead of us, was even more popular. The two of them were school celebrities. Ninomiya gave off a special aura. There was always a crowd of kids who wanted to be friends with him. When we entered middle school, he started wearing his hair tied back and making girls laugh with his jokes, but it wasn't just the girls. When Ninomiya told a joke, everyone who heard it laughed. He was always at the top of the class and took upper-level classes after school while the rest of us were struggling with our homework. None of us could keep up with him. Not even the teachers.

"Hurry up."

I stood there paralyzed and silent.

"You never learn, do you? We've been doing this how many years now?"

Ninomiya threw up his hands in disgust. His friends doubled over laughing. They couldn't get enough of this. That's when I saw Momose, standing with his arms crossed, a little behind the wall of kids.

Momose had shown up in middle school. His grades were just as good as Ninomiya's, and I heard they went to the same advanced after-school classes. I had never exchanged words with Momose. He was always with Ninomiya, but he never said much, and I never saw him get worked up like the rest of the kids. For reasons I didn't understand, he watched gym class from the bleachers. While he was no match for Ninomiya, he had a face that anyone would describe as handsome, and both of them were at least four inches taller than me. Momose always had this expression that told you nothing about what he was thinking. He never bullied me directly. He just stood off to the side, crossed his arms and stared.

"We've got places to be," said Ninomiya. "We'll have to save your masterpiece for another day. Make all three pieces of chalk disappear and you can go."

Ninomiya told the others to stick two of the pieces of chalk up my nose. He waved the third piece in front of me like a sardine and said, "Come on, Eyes, where's your please and thank you?" He kicked me right in the knee with the instep of his foot.

Whether they were kicking or punching or pushing me, Ninomiya and his friends were careful not to ever leave a mark. When I got home and saw I had no bruises, I always wondered where they could have learned this kind of trick.

They kicked me in the knees and thighs, but never hit the same place twice. One of them booted me in the chest, like he was checking to see how soft I was. They pushed me, threw me into a wall. I staggered and crashed into a desk. Happens all the time, I told myself. It's nothing. It happens. I waited for it to end.

Pulling me up by my hair, they forced the chalk up my nose and made me eat the other piece. I bit it with my front teeth.

Ninomiya and his friends just watched, laughing like crazy.

Thus far I had been forced to swallow pond water, toilet water, a goldfish, and scraps of vegetables from the rabbit cage, but this was my first time eating chalk. It had no smell or taste. They yelled at me to chew faster. I closed my eyes and broke the chalk apart inside my mouth, focusing on chewing, not on what it was. I heard it crunch. The broken pieces scraped the insides of my cheeks. My job was to keep my jaw moving and to swallow, so I swallowed. Chalk coated the inside of my mouth.

I did this for all three pieces. One of them yelled, "Lemonade! Lemonade!" and brought me a plastic cup streaked with paint and full of a dirty milky liquid. Chalk dust dissolved in water. Pushed against the wall, cup pressed into my face, I drank it all. As the liquid traveled down my throat, I felt the urge to vomit, and the next thing I knew I had thrown everything up. Tears and spit dripped from my nostrils and my eyes—dry heaving, both hands on the floor. One of the guys asked me what the hell I was doing and stepped back, but he was clapping. Cheering. They pressed my face into the mess and said, "Clean it up." Everyone was smiling, laughing.

That was the first day I wrote back to Kojima.

I had never written anyone a letter, and I had no idea what to say or how to say it, but with my freshly sharpened pencil, I wrote whatever came to mind, then erased most of it, until finally I had something I could keep. Try as I might, I could never seem to fill more than a single page. We only ever wrote about unimportant things, but over time we came to understand each other. To make sure no one saw me, I showed up at school before anyone else and stuck my note inside Kojima's desk. The morning after that, I would pick up her reply and read it in the bathroom. We never made a rule about it, but neither of us said a word about school or being bullied.

When I finished a letter, I took off my glasses and held the paper close to my left eye so I could read the words I wrote. Rereading them gave me a headache, but only on one side of my head.

I had a lazy eye.

What my right eye struggled to see was part of what my left eye saw. Because everything had its blurry double, nothing had any depth. I had a hard time touching things even when they were right in front of me. I would miss. It didn't matter if I used my fingertips or my whole hand. I was never certain that I was touching the right thing, or touching it the right way.

Hi Kojima. I read your letters a bunch today. You're using a mechanical pencil, right? I use a regular one.

To answer your last question, I guess my hobby is reading, but I don't know if I have a favorite book or type of book. Talk to you soon.

Hey hey. Thanks for your letter. It rained so hard today. It was so loud under my umbrella I thought it was about to rip. On my way home, by the Yokoyama building, a huge truck drove through a puddle and splashed water all over me. It was like something from a manga. If it was, what do you think the speech bubble would say? Maybe I suck at it, but I like writing letters. I'm excited to get your next one.

Hello. It's nighttime and the wind is blowing like crazy.

I think writing is hard. It's probably harder than talking. Maybe I'll get better if I practice. I'm trying. I've been sitting at my desk for over an hour and this is all I've managed to write. Talk to you soon.

Hey again. Thanks for your letter. My midterm came back, and I'm devastated. I barely passed! I won't ask you what you got, but I'm sure you did way better than me. Oh yeah, your speech bubble idea was super funny. If another truck rushes by and splashes me again, that's what I'm going to say!

By the way, this is my second time trying to write this letter today. The first time didn't work out, so I gave up and started sewing. Nothing too advanced, just a little cross-stitching. I really wanted to make a cushion cover, but I didn't have a cushion, so I used what I had to sew these small flower-shaped things. I really like making stuff like that. My hobbies right now are writing letters and sewing. Can't wait for your next letter.

Hi. How are you? I said in my last letter that I was having trouble writing in my own voice. I think I know why. It's my pencil.

I like 6B pencils because they almost never snap. When I was writing, I realized something. Your voice reminds me of a 6B. I'm not sure if this is going to make sense, but it's like they're soft and rigid at the same time. Almost unbreakable. Sorry for not making sense. Just thought I'd give it a try.

It's 8:30 at night. I have to do my geography homework. Bye for now.

Hello, hello, good evening. Well, I bet it's morning by the time you read this.

How's the weather over there? It's raining where I am. It's not supposed to be this rainy in May, but it is. Yeah, it's raining.

More importantly, though, how many times do I have to ask you to tell me what books you like? Is it a big secret? I've never read a whole book for fun, so I was just curious. I've read . . . let's see. Oh wait, in elementary school, I think I read some Chinese history book that we had on the borrow-a-book shelf. I can't believe I just remembered that. If I hadn't written you this letter, I would never have remembered that.

By the way, I wanted to ask you. What is it you like about reading? I forgot to ask before. Do you think it's fun? Language class is enough reading for me, but tell me if you ever find something interesting. My house is just like what you said about your house. So boring. It's funny, but when

I'm doing nothing, I get this feeling like I'm fighting some-
thing. Stuck . . . fighting. It never goes away, even when I'm
in bed, even when I'm walking around. There's a year and a
half left of middle school, but if everything goes smoothly, we
have three more years of high school after that. We'll be doing
the same thing for years. Don't you think that's weird? I do.

What do you think the future is going to be like? I think
about that stuff a lot. What if the world really ends in 1999
like everyone says? But if it doesn't, nothing's gonna change,
though, right?

Hey, I have an idea. You can tell me if you don't like it.

I almost don't want to say it, but I'm going to. What if we
met up again on the second Wednesday of next month? It was
a Wednesday the other day when we met at Whale Park. It
can be our day. If you don't like the idea, you better keep it
to yourself. Just kidding. You can tell me. Write back.

Hello. Today felt like summer. I can't believe May's
already over.

Thanks for the pad of paper, by the way. It's great. I'll use
it when I'm done with the one I'm using now.

Thanks for saying yes to meeting in the fire stairwell. I
don't know how to put it, but I think we'll be more comfort-
able up there. It's quiet, and it has a nice breeze. No one will
bother us. Just take the elevator all the way to the top. Open
the door on the right and you'll see the stairs. You'll see what
I mean. I'll be waiting there on Wednesday, two weeks from
now. I'm looking forward to it. See you soon.

I was thinking of Kojima in a completely different way.

Not like it was anything new, but it got harder and harder
for me to watch and listen to the other girls in our class bullying her, just like it was stressful knowing that Kojima watched
me being bullied. I didn't want to hear them, but we were all

in the same room, and my ears couldn't block them out. I didn't want to see it, but I couldn't keep my eyes closed.

To them, I was "Eyes." They called me over and made me do random things, or knocked me down, or made me run for my life around the track at recess while they watched me from inside. Ninomiya and his friends laughed at me, as usual, from the windows. They called Kojima "Hazmat" and said she smelled like fish or worse. I watched them send her to the store. I saw them kick her the same way they kicked me. Once, I saw them yell, "Time for a bath!" and dunk her head in the fish tank.

In her notes, Kojima was energetic and alive, an entirely different person from the girl I saw in class. Whenever I saw things happen to her, I got this sharp pain in my chest, but as bad as it hurt there was nothing I could do. I didn't want her knowing that I saw her. I had to look away, pretending not to watch.

That year, like the year before, our class had to prepare for the chorus competition and the formal assembly that came after.

A bunch of classes were cancelled in preparation for the big night, giving Ninomiya and his friends ample opportunity to bully me harder. After school and in the halls and in the schoolyard, excitement filled the air, but I was still taking orders from Ninomiya, and getting kicked in the chest. At lunch they sent me to buy them snacks. I always ate my lunch alone. So did Kojima.

"Buddy, you need to have that eye looked at." It was a Saturday, after class. We were back in homeroom, and Ninomiya was tapping my head with a ruler. "Don't worry, I'll fix you."

On any normal Saturday, the kids who weren't in clubs would have gone home by now, but today, we were allowed to stay at school and practice for the competition or work on our costumes. Ninomiya told me I was going into the locker where we kept the cleaning supplies.

"Just being around you makes me sick."

He sat down on a desk, put a black elastic in his lips, and drew his hair into a ponytail.

"Doesn't he make you sick?"

The unpopular girls he was addressing were so embarrassed that they blushed, but they smiled at him and nodded.

"You get it, Eyes? Nobody wants you around."

They tied my hands with a jump rope, stuffed a rag in my mouth, and shoved me in the locker.

"Don't go anywhere," Ninomiya said, "or you'll be in there all week."

One of the guys pushed me to make me fit. The door clanged shut.

This wasn't my first time inside a locker. I was no stranger to the dust-clogged air and muted darkness. Whenever this sort of thing happened, I just started counting in my head, not thinking about anything else. When I got to a hundred, I went back to one and started over. I never asked myself how many hundreds I had counted or how much time had passed. I tried not to think anything or feel anything or let my mind wander. Just worked my way through the numbers, saying them inside my head. But the whole time, I could hear the voices of my classmates, talking and practicing their songs. They jumbled with the voice in my own head, reciting number after number.

I couldn't tell how long I had been in there, but at some point I noticed the room was silent. I had to go to the bathroom really bad. Holding it in gave me goosebumps. I held my breath and listened closely for a voice. Nothing. It seemed like it had easily been an hour since they locked me in the locker, but it could have been two, or even more. I had no idea.

I had to pee so bad it hurt. The thought of what awful

things would happen if Ninomiya saw me leave made me consider peeing then and there, but I had to get out. I tapped the door of the locker with my toe. When I kicked it hard, the door screeched open. I squinted at the light. The classroom was deserted. I tiptoed into the hallway and looked out the windows and down onto the field. Some of the kids who had been messing around in homeroom were out there throwing a ball and yelling. I wanted to know if Ninomiya was with them, but I couldn't tell.

I slipped the jump rope from my wrists and headed down the empty hallway to a bathroom. I sat down in one of the stalls and breathed, trying to work through the knot in my stomach. What would happen if they found out that I'd left? What would they do to me? The thought kept coming back. My patience had run out. It felt like my heart wanted out of my chest. I could never get used to the burden of these questions. Maybe they would cut me some slack if I explained I had to use the bathroom. Maybe Ninomiya had forgotten I was in there and gone home. It was all that I could think about.

Trying to think about something else, I imagined what would happen the next time Kojima and I met up. I had high expectations. There were only ten more days until the day we promised to meet. I pulled out her notes and read through them again. Not all of them, which would have been impossible, but the ones I liked the most. I carried them around, as I had from the start, stuffed inside my planner. The rest of them were on my bookshelf in my room, inside the slipcase of my dictionary. I read them whenever I was in my room.

When they were stuffing me into the locker, I hadn't seen Kojima in the classroom. I wondered if she made it home okay. Her stiff-looking hair appeared before my eyes. I found myself remembering how the girls had said her breath stank during chorus practice and shut her mouth with tape. I felt pressure on my chest. I remembered how hard one of the tall girls laughed when they ripped away the tape. I even remembered what she said: "At least now your lip's clean." I sighed and put the notes away. I asked myself if Kojima ever felt this way after she saw me being bullied. It was a hard question to ask.

I heard voices approaching. Whoever they were, they came into the bathroom. I felt myself stop breathing, and I froze. I panicked, but silently unlocked the stall, so that they wouldn't see that it was locked, then pressed a hand against the door so that it wouldn't open.

Two of the guys.

At first I wasn't sure who, but in no time I recognized that one of them was Ninomiya from the way he talked. My heart was beating so hard I thought he must have heard it. To try and slow it down, I clenched my teeth. So many things spiraled through my mind. I couldn't breathe right.

Ninomiya was on the other side of the door, in here with someone else.

The other voice was almost too low to hear. I knew it was another student, but I couldn't tell who.

Ninomiya laughed. "Seriously, what a loser. Get a life."

It sounded like they had come in here to talk; neither of them used the bathroom. I heard Ninomiya say, "Like you'd know." There was something strange I couldn't place about the way he said it. I couldn't tell if he was acting cute or being mean.

The other guy replied, but I couldn't make out the words and couldn't fathom what they were discussing. The faucet squeaked. Someone washed their hands. Ninomiya laughed again.

Then nothing. Silence.

I pricked up my ears, trying to figure out what happened.

Ninomiya burst into laughter. Inside the stall, I lost touch with reality. I squeezed my eyes shut and told myself this isn't happening, I'm not here, there's nobody here. After some time, their voices faded, and I realized they had left. For a minute, I just sat there. When I was certain they weren't coming back, I rushed back to the classroom, and when I saw Ninomiya wasn't there, I grabbed my bag and ran.

The first week of June came and went, and soon it was the second Wednesday of the month. I met Kojima, as promised, at the top of the fire stairwell. When she saw me, she gave a little wave. I waved back in the same way.

I was worried I might be nervous, but for some reason I wasn't. It felt like we were back where we belonged, like the last time that we met. I couldn't tell if this was a result of all the notes, but if it was, those notes were even more powerful than I thought.

"Do you come here a lot?" she asked.

"Yeah, sort of."

The breeze made us feel light. Kojima giggled. Her cheeks had a slight rub of dirt, and her uniform was full of wrinkles. On the outside, she was the Kojima I saw in class. Her coarse hair looked like an animal on her head. Her eyebrows were low, and under them two lucid eyes were staring at me. She smiled. We stuck our heads over the railing and looked over the town. A strong breeze whooshed up at us and made Kojima giggle even more. The sound of the wind and Kojima's laughter hummed in my ears.

We sat down on different steps of the concrete stairwell and talked. It felt totally natural. Like we could talk for hours. We went back and forth, telling little stories, and they fit together. I was so incredibly at ease. Kojima looked like she was really relaxed too.

I had my notebook from language class in my bag, at Kojima's request.

"It's nothing special."

"Come on, show me." She held out her hand.

"There's nothing to see," I said. "I mean, you've seen how I write in my notes." But Kojima said she wanted to see what my writing for class looked like.

When I pulled out the notebook, Kojima snatched it from me. With her other hand, she pulled her personal notebook from her bag and tossed it in my lap.

"Let's swap."

Kojima's handwriting was just like in her notes, thin lines in mechanical pencil. She had written on and on, about all kinds of stuff. She gripped my notebook with both hands and held it open like a newspaper, bringing her face closer to see better. It seemed for a while like she was really getting into it, but then she looked up and raised her eyebrows in this cartoonish way and said, "Ah, yes. I think I understand now." She nodded a few times and started to laugh. When I asked her what she had understood, she said it was a secret, stood up, and let out a huge yawn. I could see practically the entire inside of her mouth. It was so red. I had to look away.

Somewhere far off across the sky, a bolt of thunder cracked and made room for more silence. Thunderbolt, Kojima said, three distinct syllables. Resting her chin on the railing, she turned her neck, in a slow and grinding roll, to face me. Thunder's crazy, I said.

"Hey," she said, "Remember a while ago what happened to the curtains and library books . . . and the string from the blackboard eraser? How they were all cut up?"

"Yeah, I remember," I answered automatically.

At the end of April, kids had started finding cut marks in the classroom supplies or the stuff in their own desks. For a minute, it was kind of a hot topic. It felt like it had happened a long time ago, but it hadn't even been two months. At first, they found cuts in the bottom of the curtains, but then someone found holes cut in a corner of the hamper bag the girls used for their gym clothes, and after that they found cuts in the covers of the paperbacks, and the eraser snipped from its string, and nearly an inch cut off the bristles of the broom.

Whenever someone found another clue, the class went psycho. Nothing was ever totally shredded. Just a quick snip, no more than an inch, with the tip of the scissors. All the cuts looked similar. While it lasted, the kids were desperate to find the culprit, but there was no real evidence, and no way of telling who had done the deed. Before long everyone lost interest, and in a couple of weeks they had forgotten all about it. I remembered now how scared I was that somebody might lie and blame it on me. But as much as it had haunted me at the time, it hadn't been on my mind at all until Kojima mentioned it.

"It was me."

"Seriously?" I couldn't believe it. "No one ever suspected you."

"I know." Kojima shook her head. She fixed her gaze at the toes of her sneakers. "Aren't you going to ask me why I did it?"

"Why'd you do it?"

"Nobody's forcing you to ask." She laughed it off. "I don't have a good answer anyway. It's just, I dunno, sometimes I cut things. Not just anything. Certain things. When I cut them, it makes me feel like things are finally normal."

"Normal?"

"Yeah."

"You mean it calms you down?"

"More like the opposite."

"The opposite? Like, it works you up? And that's normal?"

"No, it's not like that."

Kojima kicked the stair with her heel.

"I don't really know how to say it, but it's like something's wrong, all the time, and I can't do anything to stop it. It's always there. When I'm at home, when I'm at school. But things can be good sometimes. Really good. Like when I'm talking to you or writing letters. Those things are really good for me. Then I start feeling like everything's okay. And that makes me happy. But know what? That feeling like everything's wrong and this feeling like everything's okay, I guess a part of me wants to believe that neither one of them is, like, natural . . . I guess I want to feel like they're both exceptions to the rule. I mean, I almost never feel like everything's okay, but just because most of my life feels wrong doesn't mean that's how I want it to be. There's a part of me that doesn't feel like anything is wrong or okay. Just normal. That's the part of me I like, the normal part." She closed her lips.

"Normal."

"Yeah. It's like I'm struggling to keep things normal. Like, this is my normal. And if I don't hold onto it, it's like everything's going to fall apart, for real."

"And cutting things makes you feel normal?"

"Yeah. Like, when I'm cutting things, in my head, I keep telling myself: Okay, this is normal. And, in that moment, everything that's wrong and everything that's good, it kind of vanishes. It's like that. Like normal's coming right out of the scissors."

"But you stopped." The excitement about who had left the cut marks only lasted a few days. When the cutting stopped, it was like it had never happened.

"Yeah," Kojima said. "It was a bad idea to do it at school." She sighed. "Like, it's really personal, so I don't know if I can explain it, but doing it to other people's things where they could see me didn't feel right."

I nodded.

"At home, I usually cut paper and stuff like that, but it's never enough. It's safe, though. Still, cutting paper doesn't really do much for me. I throw it out as soon as I'm done. But what really feels good to cut, or, you know, the stuff that really works, you can't just throw away . . . it comes from things that are, you know, way more absolute, or like, important. I don't know."

I thought about this for a second.

"What do you mean by absolute and important?"

"Yeah . . . I'm not sure, actually." Kojima rubbed at the skin around her eyebrows. I could hear her fingers rub against the skin.

"What about fingernails? You can always cut your fingernails."

"Nails are nothing," she said. "You cut nails with clippers. I like scissors. I mean, you saw what I did at school, didn't you? I didn't cut everything to pieces. I only snipped the ends. And I was careful. Everything exactly the same length. It would be a waste if I'd cut things up so badly that they couldn't be used. I don't want to be wasteful."

"What do you mean?"

"Remember the curtains? I didn't cut them up so bad they couldn't be curtains anymore. Nails, though, even if you cut them, nothing changes. They grow back. I guess it sounds like that would do the trick, but it's not the same. If you don't clip your nails short enough, it's really dangerous. They'll snag on things. My grandparents let their nails go, and they got hard and cracked. When that happens, they get infected, and you end up with tetanus. Then the bacteria spreads, and it goes to your head. Like my grandparents. They started foaming at the mouth, spinning around, and dropped dead from combustion."

"Combustion?"

"You've never heard of it? I thought everyone knew about that. It's horrible. Kind of like the plague and rabies combined, I guess."

"That's how your grandparents really died?"

"Why would I make that up?" She shot me a glare that hit

me right between the eyes. "That's how they died. So you can see why nails won't work. It was a good idea, though. I need something else, something better."

We went on talking about all kinds of other things. Like the spots on ladybugs. The height of bike seats. Snow globes. Why people don't print money when they're broke. We even talked about the end of the world. It felt like we could have talked forever, but before long it was time to go. We stared in silence at the sky. Color was spreading over the west. The day was coming to an end. Raucous crows flew by, one after another, like they were chasing something down. It was hard to say goodbye. I wanted to ask if she thought we'd meet up again, but I couldn't find the words. Kojima said bye and pretended to leave but kept poking her head out. I laughed every time. The last time, she gave me a big wave and disappeared.

I met my new mom for the first time the winter when I was six. Before that, we were living with my dad's mom, my grandma, but one day, after she died, this other woman showed up at the house. My dad didn't introduce her as my new mom or explain that she was moving in. He treated having her around as normal. From then on, she cooked for us and ate with us.

She had been living with us for over a year when she looked up at me, like something was wrong, and blurted out, "You can call me Mom." We were sitting across from each other, eating some kind of sweet fish. On the TV, a mob of kangaroos was hopping toward the setting sun, and we were watching them intently. I had no idea how to respond, so I said sure, and ate my fish in silence.

Mom hadn't changed at all since then. She had the same hairstyle and hadn't gained any weight or lost it. All her skirts looked the same to me, and her socks were always folded down into even bands at her ankles.

"What?"

She was kneeling by the vacuum, wrapping up the cord.

"Nothing." I told her that finals had started along with swimming class.

"How's that going?" She sounded like she didn't care at all.

"Which one? Swimming? Finals?"

"Let's start with finals."

"Not bad. The usual."

"Not giving you a hard time?"

"Some are."

"Yeah," she said. "Just don't get a twenty. Better off with a zero!" She laughed, but she wouldn't look at me.

"It's really hard to get a zero," I said. "Though I guess on some tests, you get a zero for not writing your name."

"Well, I don't know, just give it all you've got." She stood up, leaning on the vacuum. Once you're done, it'll be summer vacation."

"I know."

She looked at me like she had just remembered something.

"You know how the cord on the vacuum has that strip of red tape at the end, to tell you when it's out? But before you make it to the red part, there's some yellow tape, too, right? What are they trying to say? Don't you think the red one is enough?"

"I guess so."

She looked like she wasn't so sure and went into the kitchen.

At the end of June, the rain came all at once. If you tried opening a window for fresh air, the moisture filled the room. Everywhere was just as stuffy as at school. During art class, Ninomiya said let's make a railroad, and told his friends to hold me down and spread my fingers while he shot staples into my palm. The little holes they left stung worse than bees. Dark clouds hung in the sky for days. The smell of rain was every-where.

Kojima and I were still leaving each other notes.

This was honestly my only source of pleasure. Using the paper she had given me, I spent hours writing my replies.

The slipcase of my dictionary was filled with notes. On nights when I found myself inexplicably disturbed and unable to sleep, or when thoughts about my future or school depleted me, I turned toward my bookshelf, without getting up, and gazed at the spine of the slipcase holding all the notes. It held the words Kojima wrote for me. My eyes were seeing double, a little pair of rectangles casting a warm light at me through the darkness. I almost felt like I could reach out and touch it. Then I started thinking about how I hoped the notes I wrote Kojima brought her comfort when she was hurting.

Hello, how are you? It's already July. It feels like we just had midterms, but here we are at finals. I can't believe it.

The other day, I tried counting all the letters we've shared over the last couple of months. How many do you think there are? Count them up and find out! It would be weird if you didn't get the same number as me. Anyway, I think you'll be surprised.

Know what's funny about letters? Unless you beg the person who you sent them to, you never get to read the letters you wrote again. Isn't that weird? Anyway, I'm taking excellent care of your letters, just in case you ever want to know what you sounded like when you were fourteen. Hey, I just thought of something good. On the second Wednesday of July 1999, whatever we're doing and wherever we are, let's meet up. We can bring all of our letters with us. Isn't that the best idea? Where should we meet? Can't wait for your next letter.

Hello. The other day at the bookstore, I looked at Nostradamus's predictions. It was just like you said. There were pictures where the sun was square, and Mary was crying tears of blood. I don't know what that has to do with the end of the world, but it definitely felt ominous. I wonder what's going to happen. It looks like people get excited like this at the end of every century. But don't worry about it either way. If the world ends, we won't be able to meet up with our letters for a reunion, but that's not our fault. Bye for now.

Hi again. I wonder what kind of person you'll be when you're twenty-two. I've been thinking a lot about stuff like that recently. Wouldn't it be amazing if we're still writing letters then?

Okay, I have a favor to ask. Actually, it's an invitation.

When the semester is over, I have something I want to show you. A place. If we don't go during vacation, we're going to miss it.

It's Heaven, the place I want to show you.

Just think about it. I think you'll love it. Please say yes.

Hey Kojima.

Well, it looks like you're intent on keeping it a secret until we go. I can't wait. Where is this place? Are you ready for finals? The math exam wasn't as bad as I expected, which is nice, but I have no idea what to do for science. If I don't make the cut, they're going to put me in remedial classes, so . . . Bye for now.

Good meowning. The only final I have left is English. But I don't know how well I did on any of the others.

We should go to Heaven on the first day of summer vacation. It can be the first thing we do this summer, the very first.

I'll be waiting for you at the ticket gate at 9:00, on the first day of vacation. See you then!

Once I had made plans to see Kojima over the summer, it was impossible for me to settle down.

I wanted to know what this Heaven place was all about and to see where she was planning to take me, but what excited me the most was that the two of us were meeting up and going off somewhere together. I had no idea what I should bring, or what to wear, or how much money I would need. What to wear bugged me most of all. I had never really given clothes much thought. I just wore whatever my mom bought me without worrying about it. My hard-won conclusion was that I shouldn't wear something that had a pattern. That didn't leave me with many options, but I spent hours on end trying to plan my outfit. I finally settled on a navy crewneck t-shirt, some jeans I'd been wearing since last year, and the Converse high tops I wore outside of school. Still, I couldn't convince myself this was the right choice. There was no one around for me to ask. But even with the clothing question solved for now, I still had to figure out the money. What I had left from New Year's and saved from my monthly allowance came to about 10,000 yen. Counting out the bills gave me a momentary confidence. I slipped the bills into my wallet and put it in my pocket, to see how it would feel. I felt bigger. I felt like I could walk tall. Yeah. I was sure that this would be enough to deal with whatever came our way. Then I went back to worrying about clothes.

On the final day of school, I read over the last note from Kojima in the bathroom and put it in my planner, like the others. Out in the hall, I stayed close to the wall, all the way back to the classroom. Ninomiya was sitting on a desk in the middle, surrounded by the others. They were laughing like crazy about something. I heard someone say something about summer school. Avoiding their line of sight and dodging the laughter, I returned to my seat as quietly as possible, taking shallow breaths, and placed my palms in the cool space inside my desk.

The bell rang. School was over, and the room surged as if a dam had broken. Kids spilled out of class the way they always did when they were free to go. I saw one of the girls kick the back of Kojima's chair on her way out. Kojima winced and shot up in her seat. For a moment she froze, but once the usual girls were gone, she gathered up her bags and slowly left the room, hands full and shoulders heavy.

I watched her go, then started packing up my bag. One of Ninomiya's friends walked by and smacked me on the back of the head. My teeth sank into my tongue. Deep. My molars bit the thick part at the back so hard it made a sound. My tongue stung to the point I thought that I could hear it pulsing. The pain tugged at the muscles of my neck. I couldn't close my mouth, but I could taste the blood in my saliva. The numbness persisted. Pain swarmed the inside of my skull. All I could do was swallow whatever filled my mouth.

Sitting motionless in the vacated classroom, I caught the sound of someone whistling, walking toward me, down the hall. My impulse was to hide under my desk, but I didn't have time.

It was Momose. I went tense. I couldn't look, but when I did, he showed no sign of noticing me. It was like Momose was alone there, whistling to himself. With his hands stuffed in his pockets, he walked over to his desk, taking every step with enviable grace.

He sat down with his back toward me and tapped his feet, keeping rhythm with his whistling. Then he leaned down and pulled a notebook from his bag and started writing. From where I sat I couldn't see what he was writing. Now and then he looked up and shook his head, then nodded to himself and set his hand in motion.

As I watched his back shift and his elbow moving, I found myself listening to whatever he was whistling. It wasn't the melody, which I didn't recognize, but the way he whistled. It was perfect, every note clear and true. Nothing was stopping me from getting up and leaving, but for some reason I didn't.

A girl said Momose's name. She was at the door. Her bangs were cut in a straight line above her eyebrows, and her dark eyes, unbelievably black, were trained directly on Momose. She was little, with a little face. She came across as too young to be in school with us. The uniform was right, but she looked nothing like any of the girls in our grade. She was so pretty I couldn't look away. She was unlike any girl I had seen in my entire life. It was weird. Her face was too much like Momose's. It looked like he had noticed her, but he went on whistling and writing in his notebook. The girl didn't seem to notice I was there. It was like I didn't exist. She went over to Momose and placed a hand on his desk. Peering at the notebook, she bobbed her head in time with his whistling and watched him write. Her long straight hair grazed his arm. She crouched and looked at him. When he was finished, they stood up, neither of them saying a word. The girl put her hand on his arm, and they left the room. Momose continued whistling, not skipping a beat.

I sat back in my chair, unsure of what to think. I couldn't believe that Momose had really been there, much less that this girl, someone I'd never seen before, had shown up out of nowhere and left with him. Entranced as I was, I lost my grip on the perfect melody Momose had been whistling. The girl's face escaped me, too.

When I finally grabbed my bag to leave, Ninomiya came into the room. I sat up straight, but Ninomiya looked distracted; when he saw the room was empty, he walked right out. A second or two later, he came back to the doorway and asked me if I'd seen Momose. I shook my head like I had no idea.

CHAPTER TWO

The next morning, I left my house with enough time to arrive fifteen minutes early. I told my mom I was heading to the big library one town over.

I was waiting nervously beside the ticket machine when Kojima showed up: 9 A.M. on the dot. Her hair was the same as always, and so were her sneakers, but she was wearing a Hawaiian shirt and a beige skirt that went down to her calves.

Far from being upstaged by her head of hair and her bunchy skirt, the Hawaiian shirt was enormous, covered with pointy leaves and red fruits that looked like mangoes. Kojima had tied the corners of the hem into a tight knot at her belly button. This was the first time I'd seen anyone wearing a Hawaiian shirt in real life, but I knew what it was instantly. When Kojima spotted me, she jogged over, waving with one hand. In the other, she had a floppy bag with a drawing of a kitten's face that almost looked like it could have been a photograph.

"You ready?" she said as she came up to me, smiling, kind of shyly. I was feeling the same way, but I put on a straight face and told her yeah. Now that she was closer, I could see the glass beads on the clip she used to pin back her bangs.

"I woke up super early," she said, scratching at her eyebrow.

"What time?"

"Four."

"Whoa," I said. "You're not sleepy?"

"No, but I was earlier," she said, "at like seven. Hey, what's wrong with your voice?" She gave me a suspicious look. "You sound different."

"I bit my tongue."

"When?" She squinted at me.

"Yesterday."

"You must have bit it pretty hard."

"Yeah," I said, "I did."

"Did it hurt?" She squinted even harder.

I said it did.

"Did you cry?"

"No," I said.

She said that if it hurt so bad I should have cried. I told her that in my opinion hurting and crying were different things.

"You think?" she said, tilting her head, then stepped back like she was startled and looked me up and down. "I've never seen you wearing anything other than your uniform. Look at you."

"I'm totally normal. Don't look at me like that," I said. "I mean, look at you."

"This?" She bent her neck to look at herself. "It's my tropical outfit."

"Cool."

"It's like, my someday best."

"Your someday best?" I asked. "What's that mean?"

"What do you mean?" she asked back. "You don't say that?"

"I don't think so . . ."

"Well, how can I put it, it's the clothing you wear on really special days."

"Oh," I laughed. "You mean Sunday best?"

"Sunday best? That means the same thing?"

"I think so."

"Whoa." She took another look at her Hawaiian shirt. I was staring at it too.

"It really feels like summer," I said.

"Yeah," she said and looked up at me in a really nice way. "It is. It was still dark when I woke up, but I knew right away that it was summer. Summer starts today."

We were waiting on a bench on the platform when the dark green face of the train rolled into the station. It made a sound like when a big animal blows air through its nose. The doors slid open in unison and, once we were aboard, the train rolled slowly ahead.

Aside from an old couple, some businessmen, and a woman with long hair, we had the car to ourselves. The train wobbled a little, side to side. Kojima and I each sat quietly, watching the world pass by the windows, but inside my heart was pounding at the thought that she and I were leaving town like this.

After a bit, I looked over at her and, so far as I could tell, she was excited too. Her face was glowing in a way it never did at school, and even brighter than the time we met up in the fire stairwell. When I looked at her, the nervousness I had been feeling burned off in the glow, and I felt an upwelling of relief. This was going to be fun.

Sitting next to her, way closer to her face than usual, I had no idea where to look and got a little flustered. Kojima didn't seem concerned about it. She looked me right between the eyes, the way she did whenever we met, and talked about all kinds of things, elaborating with her hands. When she got excited her voice got louder. I kind of liked it, but when she realized she was almost yelling, she got self-conscious and dropped into a whisper. Before long she was yelling again, and when I saw her realize it, we both laughed.

"Happamine."

"What's that mean?"

"It's, like, dopamine that comes out when you're really happy."

"Oh yeah?"

"And when you're really hurting," she explained, "that's called hurtamine."

"What about when you're lonely?" I asked.

"Lonelamine!" she laughed.

When the conversation lulled, Kojima turned and looked over her shoulder out the window, placing her hands on the bag in her lap. As if she could feel its fur, she petted the picture of the kitten with her pointer finger.

The train shot through a tunnel of houses into long stretches of farmland. We were barreling headfirst into an entire summer.

Kojima told me all kinds of stories about the cat they used to have, about how black and soft her fur was, and about the mutt they had, and how smart and nice he was.

She said when she was really little, they used to have a bunch of different animals at the house. Her real dad got a kick out of having them around.

"I liked the dog and cat, but my dad's more into little animals like goldfish, turtles, loaches, carp, things like that. We had so many."

"Where'd you keep them?" I asked.

"Well, aquariums cost a ton. We were broke then, but my dad found an enormous styrofoam tub somewhere, the kind that has a lid. We could only see in from above, but we made it into the best aquarium ever. Sometimes we walked to the store and picked out something new, like a bridge for the goldfish, or one of those spinny things. I was always making the turtle swim around the tub. Doesn't your family have any animals?"

"No," I said. "I don't think they've ever really thought about animals."

"You mean they don't like them?" Kojima asked, eyes wide. Her eyebrows jumped like they had a life of their own.

"It's not like that," I said, "at least not for me. I've never really been around animals. I'm not sure what I think about them."

"Yeah," Kojima said. "I can tell."

"But I feel like I might be able to get into them," I said. "I bet living with animals is really different from living with people. I mean, they can't talk."

"How would that be different?"

"I dunno. Like, it would actually be quiet, I guess."

"You mean how people are noisy, even when they're being quiet?"

"Sort of. People are always thinking about things. Animals seem different, just more quiet overall."

"But they bark and stuff."

"That's just barking."

"So you're not talking about actual sound?"

"I guess not."

"Okay," Kojima said. "I think I get it. It's like how when you're asleep, you dream, and even after you wake up, you have all these thoughts about what was going on in your dreams. Noisy like that. I wonder if anyone can ever actually stop thinking."

"I bet you can," I said, "at least for a couple seconds."

"If that's all," Kojima said, as she worked through a little yawn, "it's like you can't, though, right?"

The sun was warming our necks. It felt good. I looked at Kojima's face for a second. She looked sleepy. As we rode through the rice fields, the train chugged along, keeping basically the same rhythm all the way.

"Sometimes I wonder what it would be like if we didn't have words," I found myself saying.

"Yeah, I mean, we're the only ones who need them," Kojima said, looking me straight in the eye. "Dogs don't, and neither do things, like uniforms, or desks, or vases."

"You're right. Look at everything else in the world," I said. "We're completely outnumbered."

"If you really think about it," Kojima said, "it's kind of stupid. Human beings are the only ones talking all the time and making problems and everything."

She snorted. I nodded.

The train recited its script of sounds between the evenly-spaced stations. Each time we came to a halt, the conductor called out the name of the stop. When he switched off the mic, it made a ticklish popping sound that made Kojima giggle. The rich green rice fields ran together, and little houses shot up between them. Keeping pace with the train, the sharp light flickering off pointed stalks flew into streaks.

"Hey Kojima," I said. "This paradise we're going to . . ."

Kojima glared at me and shook her head.

"Not paradise. It's Heaven."

"Heaven?"

"Yeah. Heaven, with a capital H."

"Heaven," I repeated.

Kojima smiled. "That's right. But I'm not saying any more. You'll see when we get there. Sit tight."

I nodded, and Kojima nodded back like she was satisfied. In silence, we gazed out the windows at the passing scenery while the train made us wiggle.

"That thing you said earlier," Kojima finally said. "I think I know what you mean. When a desk or a vase gets scratched, it doesn't show you how it's hurting."

"Because desks and vases don't use words?" I asked. "Is that what you mean?"

"I don't know, maybe. More like, desks and vases probably don't get hurt," Kojima said. "Even when they're broken," she added softly.

"Yeah," I nodded.

"People are different, though," she said, softer still.

"Sometimes you can't see the scars. But there's a lot of pain, I think." After that, she was quiet.

She never stopped stroking the face of the kitten on her bag. I watched her silently. The train stopped at the next station. The doors opened. A few people got off, and a few more people came aboard, replacing them. Then the train rolled off again. A minute later, Kojima asked me something else, like she needed to make sure.

"Hey . . . if we keep doing this, just saying nothing, no matter what they do, think maybe we'll become things, too?"

I didn't know how to respond and stared at the floor. Light beamed through all the windows, revealing from every angle just how dirty Kojima's sneakers were. No part of them looked white.

"I mean," I said, "we won't literally turn into flowers or desks, obviously . . . but we'll be acting just like things. So basically . . ."

"Basically?" she said.

"It's like we're . . ." I started saying, but Kojima cut me off.

"We're a lot like things already." She bit her lower lip and laughed. "You and I both know it isn't true, but that's what we are to them."

Kojima messed around with her hair and stared at the kitten on her bag again. I stared at it too.

"Everyone's like that," I said. "That's the thing."

"That's the thing," Kojima said.

"Can't do a thing about it," I said, and Kojima broke into a laugh, but quietly. I started laughing too.

As the train rounded a curve, the houses outside tilted back and pulled away.

"Trouble is," Kojima said and took a deep breath, "even if we're just things to them, they won't leave us alone like actual things. We can never be like a clock on the wall." She gazed out the window. "That's the thing, right?"

She smiled at me.

"Hey, we're almost there."

Once we were through the turnstiles, we consulted a wooden signboard and followed the route it indicated, walking down the path, then turning left and heading straight. It took us to a big white building.

It was an art museum.

Inside, it was all white walls and white floors. The ceilings were really high, and there were tons of people, even though it was early in the day. They were all taking their time. Their whispers, rustling like fabric, sank into the whiteness of the walls. Paintings hung as far as I could see, each given its own warm halo of light. When we were standing in front of the first one, Kojima looked at me. Her face was alive with emotion. She stared at the painting, not saying anything, then hopped over to the next one.

I walked a little behind her, looking first at each painting and then at Kojima looking at the painting.

She would start from far away, to take the whole thing in, before edging her way closer, lips tight together. Once she had stared at it a while, she looked at me. When she looked at the paintings, lines appeared on her forehead. It didn't look like she was having fun at all. In fact, it looked like she was hurting. After she read the entire explanation on the placard by the frame, she jumped back, like something had occurred to her, and exhaled deeply, moving on to the next painting as if she were being pushed ahead.

The paintings here were mystifying.

In the reds and greens of the canvases, maidens danced with animals, a goat or something carried a violin in its mouth, and a man and a woman embraced under a gigantic blazing bouquet.

This swarm of unrelated images was like a glimpse into a

dream. But not a good one. The joy I saw there was ferocious, and the sadness suffocatingly cold. Blues thrown onto the canvas warred with yellows approaching like tornadoes. People gathered round aghast to watch a circus spin to life. Above a city of snow, a man in white robes closed his eyes and prayed. Every painting was a moment of destruction coinciding with the birth of something wonderful. Each frame contained conflicting worlds. A crowd drawn into a sun spinning like a windmill. Fish washed ashore. A leery horse with eyes more human than anyone alive. A pale maiden.

"You looking?"

I was spaced out in front of a painting when I heard Kojima's voice. When I realized what she asked me, I said yeah.

"See anything you like?"

"I don't know yet," I said. Kojima's face was even more relaxed than earlier. It was reassuring.

"So the museum is Heaven?" I asked.

"Nope," she said. "Heaven is a painting." She made a little snort and looked me in the eye. "The one I like the most."

"It's called Heaven?"

"No." She shook her head. "The artist is really good, but the titles are so boring it makes me want to cry. Here, look at this one."

She pointed at the placard by the painting. She was right. It was pretty bad up against the work itself.

"Sucks, right?"

"Kinda, yeah."

"So I gave it a better one."

"You did?"

"Yep." She laughed proudly. "Heaven is a painting of two lovers eating cake in a room with a red carpet and a table. It's so beautiful. And what's really cool is they can stretch their necks however they want. Wherever they go, whatever they do, nothing ever comes between them. Isn't that the best?"

"Yeah."

"It's the best." Kojima laughed a happy laugh.

"If you look at the room for a second, it kind of looks like any other room. But it's not. It's actually Heaven."

"Heaven the place?"

"No, the one I told you about," said Kojima cautiously.

"Do you call it that because they're dead?"

"No." Kojima spoke to me in a low voice coming from the back of her throat. "Something really painful happened to them. Something really, really sad. But know what? They made it through. That's why they can live in perfect harmony. After everything, after all the pain, they made it here. It looks like a normal room, but it's really Heaven."

She let out a sigh and rubbed her eyes.

"Heaven . . ." she said. "I had a picture of it in a book."

"Yeah?"

"Funny how the more you look at pictures, not just of Heaven, but of anything, the more the real thing starts looking fake. Here, see?"

Kojima pointed.

"They're milking a horse on the horse's face. And the horse has a necklace."

"Look at these colors," I said. They were warm, but not necessarily comforting. A giant face and giant colors. We looked at the painting together.

"Look at these eyes," she whispered. "See the white line connecting the horse and the green guy?"

Eyes. The instant the word left her lips, I almost had a heart attack.

Kojima kept staring at the painting.

A little behind us, a boy who looked like he could barely walk let go of his mother's hand and ran off, bumping into Kojima's leg. He fell and started crying really loudly. Kojima was startled by the sound and tensed all over. The mother grabbed the child by the hand and pulled him up, bowing and apologizing to Kojima. She didn't seem to know how to respond and bowed back to the woman. She watched the mother lead her child out of the gallery. Once they were gone, she let out a breath and looked at me with the same startled eyes.

I wanted to say something that would make this sad and difficult expression go away, but before I had the chance she was back over by the paintings, and I joined her without saying anything.

After a while, I finally asked her.

"Where's Heaven? Farther inside?"

When she turned to look at me, I felt like I could see my own face before my eyes.

"Yeah, it's all the way in the back." She was speaking so softly. "But I'm getting kind of tired. Let's take a break."

We went outside. Kojima sat down on one of the benches and wouldn't move or speak.

When I said I was going to get us something to drink, she said she wasn't thirsty, so I walked over to the vending machines and came back with something for myself. The sun was at a high point in the sky. Just sitting there, I could feel the sweat forming in my armpits and around my neck. The skin under Kojima's nose was glistening with sweat. From where we sat, we could see onto a big open lawn slightly above us, where families and couples sat and ate their lunch on picnic sheets. Others were tossing a ball around, and some had even taken off their shirts and lay on the ground sunbathing. There were big trees growing in the field, and people leaned against them, reading. This was the height of summer, I told myself. From the edge of the horizon, the sky was generously blue. Kojima sat completely still, gripping the kitten bag in her lap. I took a sip of my drink and realized I wasn't thirsty either.

"Is something wrong?" I asked, unsure of what to say. Kojima slowly shook her head a bunch of times, then shook her head again, as if she'd missed one. I nodded and looked at the people on the grass. Looks like a painting, I thought. All kinds of people walked past our bench. I wiped my forehead with the back of my wrist.

After some time had passed, I asked Kojima if she thought we should head home. She didn't answer, other than shaking her head again.

"Unhappamine?" I asked, trying to speak her language, but she didn't say anything. I wished I hadn't said it. Now all I could do was sit there.

Eventually I realized she was crying.

Not out loud. Kojima turned away from me and pawed her eyes. Tears dripped from her palms onto her cheeks. I squeezed the bottle of my drink, lukewarm by now, and stared down at the ground. I tried to think of something I could say to her, crying silently beside me, but came up empty, unable to act on my feelings.

"It's not one thing," she finally said, in a low voice. She rubbed her cheeks with her palms, and in a voice almost too soft to hear, she said she was sorry.

"We came all this way," she said, smiling at me awkwardly, trying to hide that she was crying, but she still looked like she was crying.

Her eyes were red, and the snot dripping from her nose was sucked in and dribbled out as she breathed. The pin holding back her springy bangs looked like it would pop out any second. I noticed Kojima had a bean-shaped spot on her right cheek where her skin had lost its color. I'd never been this close to her before. I couldn't believe how vulnerable she looked. She had no fight in her, like some tiny, helpless creature waiting to be snatched away. I knew that I was helpless too, but beside me on that bench, Kojima looked smaller than any little kid I had ever seen. Much weaker than the way she looked at school. I felt incredibly sad. Unable to do more than sit and stare, I was just as helpless.

I couldn't figure out the real reason she was crying, so we just sat there quietly, together. Kojima stroked the kitten on her bag the same way she had when we were on the train. Maybe it was a nervous tic. She looked up, as if the worst was over, and stared into the sky.

"When it's this nice out, something keeps me from moving."

The July sky was saturated with summer. Nothing moved over our heads.

"I feel trapped," she laughed.

"Like there's a lid on top of you," I said.

Kojima slipped a hand into her bag and pulled out a packet of tissues. She asked if she could blow her nose. I said sure. I was surprised by how loudly she blew it.

"Good thing I had these," she said, wiping her nose. "It feels so good to really let it out, you know?"

"I'm glad."

"I don't usually carry tissues."

"Yeah."

"Glad I had them today."

"Yeah."

"Do you wanna blow your nose, too?" she asked.

"I'm fine for now," I said. I looked at my pockets. "I never carry anything. Just my wallet."

"What about your favorite pencil? Not even that?"

"I couldn't write anything down if I only had a pencil."

"But that's why everyone carries little notebooks, right?"

"My pockets aren't big enough for a notebook."

"Yeah," Kojima said, "I don't have that much on me, either." She opened her bag so I could see. "Just my wallet, my tissues, and my scissors."

"You have your scissors on you?"

I must have looked surprised. Kojima nodded sheepishly.

"Wait, though," she said, "it's not like that. I don't cut things anymore."

"No, you can cut anything you want. I'm just surprised. I didn't think you'd bring scissors into a museum."

"It's not like I brought them because we were coming," she said, a little embarrassed.

"No," I said. "Sorry."

"I always have them, outside of school . . . not like I'm gonna use them. They're just good to have. It's not like they make me feel safe or anything. I just like having them." She closed her bag and rolled the top down a couple times, then set it on her lap again.

"I know," she said. "It's weird."

She covered her mouth with both her hands and smiled nervously. We could hear girls and guys cheering from the lawn. Several bicycles whooshed past us. A sharp light flashed into my eyes, making me squint, and when I looked I saw that someone on the far edge of the lawn was laying out a silver picnic sheet.

I thought for a second, but then I said it.

"Kojima, get your scissors out."

"Why?"

"Cause."

"But why?" Little wrinkles formed between her eyebrows.

"Because," I laughed.

"Why are you laughing?" She looked puzzled. "Stop."

"Sorry," I giggled, "I'm not laughing at you."

"Then why are you laughing?" she asked sternly, with the same puzzled look.

"I'm not laughing."

"Yeah you are."

"Yeah, because you're not listening to me."

"You're not listening to *me* . . . what do you want them for?"

For a minute we were quiet, staring at the toes of our shoes. My feet were noticeably bigger than hers. I started thinking about how weird feet are. Such a strange shape. As I was staring at her shoes like that, she toed the ankle of my shoe, so I did the same to her. We did that a bunch of times, then she pressed hers right against mine and said, "Yours are so big." I laughed and said it's cause I'm a boy. She said I was right, and then we were quiet again.

"If you want to, you can cut my hair," I said, breaking the silence. "You know what you said before? Like, if you start to feel the normal slipping away. If that happens, you can cut my hair."

Kojima stared at me with her jaw hanging open.

"Your hair? Why?"

"No reason. Just thought that you might want to."

"What do you mean by your hair, anyway? Like, where?"

"Anywhere. I mean, as long as you don't cut a ton. Actually, it's fine if you do, as long as it still looks like my hair."

Hearing this, Kojima stroked the back of her left hand with the fingers of her right. She looked like she was about to speak, but something was holding her back.

"When you feel like everything's falling apart, or feel like things are too good to be true," I said, "when things get that way, you can cut my hair. Instead of cutting up the junk mail or whatever when nobody else is home. Just let me know, and you can cut it, whenever you want."

Kojima stared at me. Sweat seeped from every pore on her face. It made her skin look swollen. It was almost noon and only getting hotter. The sky was free of clouds, and there wasn't any shade in sight. Occasionally a breeze blew through the park, grazing the edges of our bodies. Then Kojima looked at me and nodded as if letting go of something big.

Following the nod, she kept her head down and carefully opened the bag in her lap. Even more carefully, she slipped her right hand into the bag and pulled out her scissors. Her nest of hair was hiding her face, making it impossible to see her expression. Now that she held the scissors, she turned her gaze to them. The handle was yellow plastic, and the tips were blunt, for crafts. The blades were flecked with different colors of paint. They looked like they had seen some heavy use.

"I've had them since the first year," she said after a while, looking at the blades.

"Of middle school?"

"No, elementary school."

"Whoa, eight years ago?"

"Are you sure it's okay?" Kojima asked me quietly. "You're really okay with me cutting your hair?"

"Yeah, a hundred percent sure."

She held the scissors with her right hand, but clasped the silvery blades with her left palm, staring at her hands, like something else was on her mind.

"Chop-chop!" I said, trying to be funny. I sat up straight with my hands on my knees and turned my back to Kojima.

She didn't move at first, but then I felt her hands in my hair.

She slipped a finger behind my ear and made a little bunch, shaking it a few times to make it the right size. The hand holding the scissors hovered behind my head. I felt my hair slip between the blades. They sliced through the clump of hair and made a grinding sound. I got goosebumps, and Kojima made a sound almost like a sigh.

I turned around to see her with her head down, holding a fistful of my hair in one hand and the scissors, slightly parted, in the other. She had cut close to the scalp, freeing a clump almost an inch thick and four inches long. The two of us sat just like that, completely still.

Without looking at me, Kojima brushed the fistful of hair across my face.

"That tickles!" I said and laughed.

She blushed and shot me a look back, like she was upset, or maybe she was happy, or maybe embarrassed, or on the verge of tears. Honestly, I had no idea what kind of face this was, but she was laughing.

"Okay . . ." But she just looked at me, still red, then looked away, then back at me. She was still holding the hair up near my mouth, so I pretended to eat it. When Kojima saw this, she laughed out loud, and I laughed too.

"There's a lot left," I said, "you can keep going." I ran a hand through my hair and touched the spot where her scissors had been. Obviously I couldn't tell the difference from before, but she was holding a fistful of my hair.

Kojima stared at the little clump of hair, then wrapped it in one of her tissues. When she was about to put it in her bag, I asked her what she did with all the other things she cut. She said she tossed them.

"Okay," I said, "then toss it. It has to be the same."

Kojima looked confused. "But it's not the same."

"Yes it is," I said. "It's nothing special."

But Kojima looked unsure. She stared at the fistful of hair.

"It's okay," I said. "When I say so, open your hand."

"I can't."

"Sure you can," I said. "Nothing's wrong. You can cut more whenever you want. There's plenty."

Kojima clenched her fist. Dead still.

"I can't do it."

"Yes, you can."

She looked uneasy, but when I said her name she spread her fingers, almost out of reflex. The color returned to her hands and she gasped. Before she realized what was happening, the tissue opened and the cluster of hair fluffed apart and tumbled to the ground, where the clippings scattered and dis-appeared.

We didn't go back into the museum.

On the ride home, we played word games. Kojima started feeling a little better, and I managed to make her laugh a few times. We were starving, as we hadn't eaten anything all day, and could hear each other's stomachs grumble. It sounded like our bellies were harmonizing. I made a joke about it, and we both laughed. But the closer we got to our stop, the less we spoke. We weren't even really looking out the windows. We sat in silence, only moving when the train moved us.

Outside the station, things were back to usual in the worst way possible. The sunset stretched over us in the distance, the shadows around us growing longer. It felt like the summer that surrounded us when we were in the park was not what we found here. Not even close, not even a little. Sweat chilled our skin in private, underneath our shirts. Our bodies were becoming tense. We didn't need to say it. She knew it and so did I.

Kojima said goodbye and waved. I said goodbye. She looked back as she walked away, disappearing around the corner.

Standing there alone, I looked all around me. There I was, at the start of summer, standing right in the middle of it, in the same place I had met up with Kojima that morning. I knew it was the same place, but it didn't feel the same.

CHAPTER THREE

D uring the first week of summer, I finished all the work I had to do over vacation, so I had nothing left. I spent almost all day reading in my room. I never went anywhere.

When it was time to eat, my mom called me down and we ate together, same as always. Dad almost never came home. When he did, he didn't stay for long.

Without school, I could get by without seeing anyone or being seen by anyone. It was like being a piece of furniture in a room that nobody uses. I can't express how safe it felt never being seen. I knew the peace could never last, but it was immensely comforting to know that, if I never left my room, no one in the world could lay a finger on me. The flip side was I had no way of engaging with the world, but that was how it had to be.

I entertained an incredible scenario where Ninomiya and his friends had somehow forgotten all about me.

When summer was over, I would show up at school to find their memories of me erased. My arrival would provoke no feeling or emotion, nothing. Something would have happened to them over the break. They would be entirely different people, no longer interested in me at all. I knew that it was cruel to be so optimistic, but, in my solitude, I couldn't resist the urge and spent entire days basking in idiotic fantasies, sometimes verging on prayer. The longer I stayed in the house the more that everything at school felt like a fragment of some story

I had stumbled upon when I was young. As if none of that had anything to do with who I had become.

Mom and I always ate with the TV on.

Every day offered a seemingly endless supply of incidents and accidents, which the news served up in a digested form. Court decisions, celebrity engagements, approval ratings, agreements. People were murdered. Tornadoes touched ground. All kinds of things.

One day, there was a story about a bullied middle-schooler who had killed himself.

A single spotlight fell onto a sheet of paper, and a solemn voice read an excerpt from his diary that sounded like a suicide note. When the voice-over was finished, the principal of his middle school and other concerned parties expressed their crippling guilt and bowed toward the camera, which cut to interviews with fellow students, their faces blurred. His family and his teachers and his classmates all claimed not to have noticed anything was wrong. What had they done to him— what made him do it? According to the program, they stole his things and shook him down for money, but the worst part was how violently they beat him.

If I turned off the TV, the news would go away, but life as I knew it wouldn't change. There was no way for me to make my life go away. My thoughts made me want to scream at the top of my lungs, but I managed to bottle up the feeling and forced myself to acknowledge that I didn't have it half as bad as the kid who killed himself. But that made me feel worse than ever. What could be more callous than using a suicide to make yourself feel better? Pretending to feel better wasn't going to solve anything. Not if I was just pretending.

At times like these, I tried hard to believe that just like summer had an end, the school year and every other year would have an end, and so would the bullying that was ruining my life. But I'd be lying if I told you that I felt any better.

My eye was behind all my problems.

I could finish school and change my surroundings, but as long as my eye was lazy, I couldn't rightfully expect any substantial change. It was more likely that things would get much worse, or maybe they already were, and I hadn't yet realized the extent of it. Maybe I would kill myself like that kid from TV, or maybe someone else would kill me first. Maybe I was already dead. These ideas flooded my mind to the point where I wasn't sure what I was thinking. I was numb with a mix of fear and nausea.

I stood in front of the mirror and studied my own face. My right eye drifted, watching something it kept to itself. It was disgusting. I leaned into my reflection. No matter how close I got, I couldn't make my eyes meet. My bad eye was like a slimy deep-sea fish from a hidden world, but it was sitting right there, lazy as ever.

Walking beside me, like on the day we visited the museum, had Kojima felt embarrassed to be seen with me? Maybe that's why she and I never talked at school. I wondered how she really felt about my eye, and what she thought of me. I can't tell you how many times I've asked myself that.

But what about me?

How did I feel about Kojima? How come I never spoke to her at school or even attempted eye contact? Sure, I was scared of Ninomiya, but what exactly made me scared? Was I afraid of getting hurt? If that was it, if that was what was haunting me, why couldn't I stand up to him? What does it mean to be hurt? When they bullied me and beat me up, why couldn't I do anything but obey them? What does it mean to obey? Why was I scared? Why? What does it mean to be scared? No matter how much I thought about it, I wasn't going to find an answer.

I tried to let these feelings pass, and when I got tired of reading books or thinking about other things I leaned against the wall and let myself space out. I took off my glasses and rubbed my eyes. I rubbed them hard. The books lining my bookshelf and the legs of my desk doubled treacherously, and it was as if my nose stopped working. I unzipped my pants and pulled out my penis. With a firm grip, I moved my hand back and forth, and I came into a balled-up tissue. This made me feel, at least for a little while, like I was bigger than my nerves. I wrapped the cummy tissue in another tissue and placed it at the edge of the bed, to flush later. I only did it when I felt burdened by these inexplicable but frequent surges of anxiety. I didn't want the things that made me feel safe or happy getting mixed up with that. I couldn't tell you why, but when I was doing it, I never once thought about Kojima. I couldn't if I tried.

Sometimes I heard my mom using the vacuum cleaner or washing dishes, but she never came into my room unannounced. The sounds travelled to me through a fissure in the outer reaches of the world. I listened to them with my eyes closed, like someone counting clouds, simply noticing their presence. Shrunken after coming, I sank forever into the mattress. I surrendered to the abyss, pressing through the carpet and the floor and the ceilings of a dozen floors below me, eternally. When I grew tired of this feeling, I sat myself up and put my penis in my underwear and opened the window to have a look outside. I could see all kinds of things from my window, but nothing could see me. The hulking summer, just like me, had barely taken its first step. I wondered what Kojima would be doing on a day like this.

Once it was late August and Obon was behind us, the end of summer was in sight.

Mom kept acting like she had something to tell me, but she would never spit it out. Sometimes we sat together and watched TV. One day, when she asked me to go down and check the mail, I saw some little kids, some in bathing suits, some naked, splashing around in a kiddie pool. Screaming and whipping the hose around.

I wanted to see Kojima again.

There were ten days until school.

The thought of it made me feel insane. I considered calling her house (her number was probably in the class directory that they had handed out in our first year), but she could have done the same. Right? I figured if she wanted to talk, she would have called me herself. I couldn't do it. But what if, this very second, she was thinking the same thing as me, waiting for me to call her? What then? Since I was thinking in circles, I tried remembering the last time that we met, recalling as many details as I could. Like when she cried, or when she held my hair in her hands and cut it off. How dry the dirt around us was, or how the asphalt felt to walk on. That little clump of hair. This made me realize how intimate the day had been. It made my chest hurt. Looking back on all these moments we had shared, I knew I wasn't wrong to want to talk, but I couldn't just call her house.

I thought over all kinds of different plans but settled on looking up her address in the directory and going to her house. From there I'd find a place to wait for her to leave and give her a head start. Once we were down the street, I could pretend to run into her, by coincidence, and call her name. It was the perfect plan.

Kojima's house was in the neighborhood beyond the tree-lined street. That familiar terrain forced me to think about school. Ten days from now, my head would be in a different place—almost definitely a worse one. It felt like I'd be walking up and down this street forever. I slapped my cheeks a bunch of times and took a few deep breaths, feigning resilience. I kept on walking.

I followed the route I had looked up on a map and reached

my destination with almost no trouble. It wasn't hard finding her house. Set apart from its neighbors, it was made from stately bricks the color of roasted tea. The nameplate on the gate was cut from a thick slab of beautiful stone. I had never seen anything like it. The more I looked at it, the less it seemed like something for a house. More like a tiny gravestone. Beyond the gate were two rows of trees with snaky trunks whose name I didn't know. At the end of the trees stood a solid three-story building, with white lace curtains in every window. It wasn't exactly new, but it didn't look old either. You could tell that it had cost a lot of money. It wasn't what I was expecting.

I hid where I could see the entrance and scoped things out. My sweat made my glasses slip. I kept pushing them back onto my nose, but they just slid down again.

It felt like I had been standing there forever, but it had probably been less than ten minutes. Standing there made me realize how stupid my plan had been. I was sweating from the heat, but a nastier sweat, unrelated to the weather, oozed over my skin and mixed with the normal kind. It started to feel like, somewhere behind me, somebody was watching me snoop around. Nervousness filled my stomach like a gas, climbing up my throat and threatening to choke me. It ran down my arms and made my hands sting. Pretty soon I couldn't stand it anymore and got the hell out of there.

First off, I had no idea what Kojima did all day and no clue what time she left the house. What was I doing showing up like this so unprepared? I had a chance to think things over as I walked. Just before I took the turn, I kept looking over my shoulder but was relieved to see nobody behind me. I was lucky I hadn't run into her. How could I explain why I was in her neighborhood, where I had never been before and would never be again? Dammit. The more I thought about it, the worse my thoughts hopelessly tangled. When I had made it past the school and onto the tree-lined street, I was over-whelmed with relief. I felt like I needed to sit down. My thighs were cold in my pants. But I just stood there.

Kojima called me two days later.

The phone rang the first time in the morning. Mom picked up but Kojima must have hung up a second later.

"No one there," Mom said, like she was talking to herself. She hung up too and went into the kitchen. She told me lunch was in the fridge and that she had a couple of errands to run, then left the house. I looked in the fridge and found a cold plate of noodles wrapped in plastic. I didn't really feel like eating, so I spaced out on the couch. That was when the phone rang again. It was Kojima.

I knew it was her from the way she said hello, but I couldn't seem to talk right. She said hey and I said hey back. For a little while, we just listened to the white hiss on the line. Kojima said, "Phones are kind of awkward," and I said, "Yeah, but they're also kind of fun." Then she said something else, and I said something too. My voice sounded nothing like me. Kojima commented on this, and I said something else that made her laugh, and we made plans to meet before school started up again.

"How about tomorrow?" she asked. I said sure. We decided to meet in the fire stairwell. Before we hung up, I asked her whether she had called that morning. She said it must have been somebody else.

After a month without seeing her, I thought Kojima looked a little different. Her hair was as unruly as ever, and her brown dress looked kind of like an apron with baggy sleeves. Her thin arms were as dark as her face. She stood there on the landing, in the same old sneakers, sticks for legs.

"How have you been?" she asked me.

"Fine. You?"

"Okay," she said.

I stood next to her and looked out over the town. Despite having taken the elevator, my whole body was sweating just from walking down the hallway. I wiped the sweat from my forehead with a handkerchief. Casually, like it was no big deal, I took a step closer, to be beside her, but the way I moved felt anything but casual. Kojima had a sweaty forehead too. I almost wiped it for her with my handkerchief. I was unbelievably nervous. I felt guilty, even criminal, for letting my curiosity get the better of me and going all the way over to her house.

Cicadas screamed in chorus out of sight, pinning the heat down around us.

We talked about what we did over the summer. I told her I didn't go anywhere, just stayed in the house and read. She asked me what I read. I gave her a few of the titles I could remember. "Were they good?" Kojima asked. "Not all of them," I said. "You make it sound like homework," she said and laughed. It made me laugh too. Then she told me how she had spent time near the ocean for a whole week.

"You have grandparents there or something?" I asked.

Kojima shook her head and said she had been visiting her real dad. "I thought I told you about him."

"Only a little."

"He's been living on his own forever," she said. "My parents got divorced when I was in fourth grade. That's when I moved here with my mom. I wanted to stay with my dad, but he didn't have enough money. There was other stuff, too, but that was basically why they got divorced, I guess. But maybe we shouldn't talk about this. I haven't seen you in so long."

"No, it's fine," I said. "You can say anything you want."

When I said that, Kojima stretched her lips. She folded her hands on the railing and used them as a pillow for her chin.

"My dad had this workshop, but it got shut down around

the time I started elementary school. We were in debt and really poor. Like, I could feel it, every day of my life. We never had enough money."

Kojima scratched at her the side of her nose with her pointer finger.

"No matter how hard he worked," she said, "it really didn't matter. He worked and worked, but nothing got better . . . seriously, I really think this is too depressing to talk about right now."

"No it's not," I said. I rested my chin on the railing just like she did and let her continue.

She looked at me, like she was thinking something over, but then she went on, more quietly.

"My dad's the sweetest guy ever. He doesn't talk a lot, but he's super nice. It's not like it's his fault that the workshop closed. But he blamed himself, for everything, like it was his responsibility. Only it wasn't. He worked all the time, day and night, but he never complained about it, not even once. When we were together, he'd always smile and everything. He'd look at me and go, 'You good?' like a bazillion times a day. Maybe it was a joke to him or something, but I'd just smile back. Then I'd go to school, feeling really good. Even at my old school, some kids made fun of me for being poor, but it never bothered me. I would just bleach my handkerchief, like every day, and iron my uniform twice a week, so it never had a single wrinkle, and every Sunday I cleaned my sneakers. We never had money, but I didn't let it get to me. I even braided my hair. You can look as good as anyone else. It doesn't even matter if you're poor. Wait, is your family rich?"

"We live in an apartment. I think we're pretty normal."

"Does your mom work?"

"No, she stays home."

"That's nice," Kojima said, but only just to say something. She scratched the side of her head. "Know what though? I think that means you're rich."

"Seriously?"

"Yeah," she said. "My mom doesn't work either, not anymore. Back then, though, she was so fed up with how things were, she started getting into arguments with my dad. Except he wasn't much of a talker. He would kind of close up when things got heated. It wasn't really arguing. More like yelling. My mom was always calling my dad names, but he never said anything back, or maybe he couldn't. But my mom didn't like that either. Well, I don't know. It's just, it kind of makes arguing hard when the other person doesn't say anything back. So she would lose it, and start crying and screaming, all the time. Eventually she started throwing things, whatever was around, saying everything was his fault, punching him and kicking him. It was crazy to watch. She went at him with everything she had. The way she cried was crazy, too. I remember feeling like it was all because we had no money. But I know it wasn't just that. Not like I get it. That's just how things were. My mom even stopped going to her job. We were all out of money and our family was falling apart. Like, we had no idea what we were gonna do next.

"I remember one time when my mom and I were sitting on one of those concrete blocks in the parking lot near where we used to live. It was like she wasn't even in there.

"It was a beautiful day, and the breeze felt amazing. That morning, we brought the laundry in together, and I told her I was gonna go pogo. You remember pogo sticks? When I came back, though, they were at it again. This time it was really bad. She threw a teacup at him and got him right on the forehead. He was bleeding. It was my cup, and it had this drawing of, like, a green gourd on it or something. But the weird thing was how, after it hit my dad and fell, it didn't break. It just rolled across the floor, right to me. Then, I swear, it rolled back upright, on its own. I can see it perfectly. I'll never forget that, ever."

"Whoa," I said.

"My dad just stood there, no reaction. He wouldn't say anything. My mom was crying, totally exhausted. Then she just walked out. As soon as she was gone, I had this horrible feeling, so I told my dad to stay put and ran after her. She was wearing her red apron, totally out of it, and sitting on those blocks. You know those concrete things they have in parking lots? I ran over to her and sat down right next to her, but she was in her own world. I kept calling her, like Mom, Mom, Mom. Nothing, though. I yanked her arm, but she barely moved. I started to panic, thinking I'd better go get my dad, but decided against it. I slapped her knee as hard as I could, crying like crazy. Going Mom, Mom. But that didn't do anything, either. It was like she couldn't even hear me. I was so scared, thinking what I'd do if she lost her mind and never said anything ever again. That was about the time that everyone in class was doing sun dares. Did you do those? Know how if you stare at the sun, you go blind? Someone decided that if you stare straight at the sun for thirty seconds without blinking, you get to make a wish. So I did it right there, sitting next to my mom, crying. Give me my mom back. I was looking straight up, right at the sun, my eyes all the way open. It was a really sunny day, too. Not a single cloud up there. The sun was really bright, white hot, like today. I still remember how painful it was to keep looking. But I kept telling myself, I can lose my sight, but I can't lose my mom. I had no idea how long thirty seconds was, but I held it. I could feel my eyelids shaking, and tears were pouring out of my eyes. I fought with everything I had to keep them open. I had been at it for a really long time when I heard my mom say, 'It wasn't supposed to be like this.' Actually, I didn't really hear her words, but I was so relieved to hear her speak. Then she said it again, 'It wasn't supposed to be like this.' I didn't know what to say back, so I just kept quiet. She was like, 'We have nothing . . . nothing.'

But she wasn't talking to me. It was like the words were just coming up, from some place deep inside her, on their own."

Realizing how long she had been talking, Kojima stared off into the distance. For a while we just sat there with our chins resting on the railing, gazing out over the town.

"When your dad's work was going well," I asked after a while, "were things okay at home?"

Kojima exhaled through her nose and looked at me.

"Not really. It didn't matter how hard he worked. Looking back on it, there were a lot of bad things going on, but I loved living with him. It didn't matter that we were poor. I mean it. I felt that way even when we were going through the worst of it. People who don't know what it's like being poor are always like, 'It's okay to be poor, as long as you have love,' but they don't know what they're saying. Honestly, I think my mom had had enough of him, like it would have been impossible to stay together. We had three terrible years like that before my aunt, my mom's sister, got involved. In the end, they decided to end things, and they got divorced."

Kojima dabbed at her lips as she spoke.

"I still don't know why my aunt had to get involved. Even after they decided to get divorced, my dad never said anything to her. It wasn't the kind of situation where you need someone to step in and settle things. But while they were getting divorced, my mom was already seeing her new guy. She never told me that, but I'm sure of it. I'm positive."

I nodded.

"One time, way, way before things went bad, my mom and I were eating dinner, just the two of us. And she started talking about my dad. Then we started talking about why they got married. It just came up, kind of naturally. Well, I guess I was the one who brought it up, but I don't really know why. So I just asked. Why? And when I did, my mom put down her chopsticks, looked at me, and said 'I felt sorry for him.' That's what she told me. She felt sorry for him. That really shook me. Then we went back to eating, like everything was normal, but I couldn't stop thinking about what she told me. When we were clearing the table, I asked, 'What made you feel sorry for him?' She answered right away. 'Everything about him.'"

Kojima paused again.

"That got me thinking, about what it really means to feel sorry for someone. Like, I thought I knew what it meant, but maybe I don't, you know?"

"Me neither," I said.

"My mom completely changed when she got remarried. We were suddenly rich, but not through any effort of my mom's. She just married someone who had money, and thought it was the coolest thing. She started acting like everything that had happened up till then literally belonged to another life. If I even mentioned my dad, it ruined her mood. I don't know . . . it felt like she was so done with everything that had happened, she was, like, overdoing it intentionally, to make a point. My dad is still alive, and so am I, but she acts like it's all in the past . . . like, I guess my mom's in a weak position at home, and she's stuck with me for good, and maybe that's why she doesn't want to make problems, which I get, but this new guy is horrible. I'm not just saying that because I hate him— even though I do. It's just, his face is so gross. Like, really. He makes this face like he doesn't understand anything that matters. But that's my life now."

She went on without waiting for me to comment.

"For part of the break, I went to my dad's house, to visit. I told my mom about it forever ago, and I don't think she was happy about it, but she still let me go. It made me so happy. My dad's working in a spa town now, with people who give massages. He doesn't give the massages, but he drives the massagers around to hotels and keeps track of their pay and everything. When I got to the station, my dad came to pick me up.

I hadn't seen him in so long that neither of us knew what to say, but it didn't take long for things to go back to normal."

"You had a good time?" I asked.

"When my dad was at work, I'd wait at home or go for a walk. When he came home, we watched TV and ate together. He has a tiny room, with a little black TV. After dinner, we'd go to the bathhouse down the street to clean up. He even asked someone from work if he could borrow an extra mattress and stuff because he knew I was coming. Whenever the phone would ring, he had to go to work, so he unplugged the phone for two days, just for me. We went to this big supermarket, and a bookstore, and all these stores and looked at everything. Furniture and electronics, stuff like that. My dad was wearing the same work clothes every day. His shoes were so worn out. I couldn't stop thinking about it, but my dad was grinning like he was super happy. As we walked around and talked, I stopped thinking about it. Then, at the pet shop, looking at puppies and kittens, my dad started talking about the loaches and carp we used to have. He was kind of surprised, I think. He couldn't believe that I remembered everything. Then he was like, why don't we go somewhere and sit down for a bit? I said, let's just go home, but he was like, it's fine, it's fine. So we went to this cafe place. He told me I could eat as much cake and drink as much soda as I wanted. He was like, let's have a party! He had this huge smile, so I said okay and had two pieces of cake, even though I don't really like it. One slice of shortcake and one of cheesecake."

A gust blew straight through the stairwell. There was nothing in the sky that spread before us for the wind to catch. It was empty, except for way off in the distance, where the last of the clouds remained.

"Hey," Kojima said to me. "Do you think there's a God?"

She had been quiet for a few minutes when she whispered this question.

"God?" I asked. "What kind of god?"

"The almighty kind. A god that knows everything. A god that knows everything about everything. You know, who can see through everything, through our lies, and really understands us."

"Do you?" I asked her, deflecting. "You think there's a god like that?"

She wouldn't look at me.

"I mean," she said, "it doesn't really need to be a god, but if there's nothing like that, then there are a whole lot of things that make no sense. Like money. My dad worked so hard, and not for his own sake. He did it for his family. But it didn't matter how hard he worked. He still ended up living alone, and it's not like he ever wanted to be rich or anything, but he's so poor now he can't buy himself new shoes, and my mom and I have gone on without him, living in luxury. How else could that happen? It's so stupid, I can't even begin to understand it. I have to believe there's some kind of god, who sees everything that happens and understands the meaning of everything we've been through when everything is over."

I didn't know how to answer her.

"When everything is over? You mean while we're alive, or after we die?"

Kojima raked the hair from her face and answered me slowly, dwelling on each word.

"We'll understand some things while we're alive and some after we die. But it doesn't really matter when it happens. What matters is that all the pain and all the sadness have meaning."

Once she had spoken, she was silent, and I tried to follow her lead, silently. I pinched my sweaty shirt away from my back, letting my skin feel the breeze.

She lifted her chin from her hands and gripped the railing firmly, hoisting herself up. Now she looked at me.

"Why do you think they do it? Why do you think they treat us like they do?"

I couldn't look at her.

My chest was thumping. I could feel my heart racing. I swallowed all my spit.

"Know what I think?" she said. "They aren't even thinking. Not at all. They're just doing what they've seen other people do, following blindly. They don't know what it means, or why they're doing it. You and me, we're just an outlet for them."

Kojima sighed.

"But it isn't meaningless. When it's all over, we'll reach a place, somewhere or something we could never reach without having gone through everything we've gone through. Know what I mean?"

Her voice was confident.

"The other kids, the rest of our class, they don't understand anything. They have no idea what anything means. They don't know how they make other people feel, and they've never stopped to think about other people's pain. They're just following along, doing what everyone else is doing. At first, I was so angry. Really. I was only making myself dirty as a way of staying close to my dad, so I wouldn't forget him. It was my own sign, a sign that I had been with him. Something that no one else can understand. A sign that my dad was out there somewhere, wearing the same old shoes, and that I was with him. Being dirty can mean something, too. But the other kids, they'll never understand that. Know what I mean?"

I nodded.

"Just like they'll never understand your eyes," she said. "Before I wrote you a letter for the first time, I read about lazy eyes in a book. I wanted to know. Like, does it hurt? How do you see the world? There are all kinds of things in the world I don't understand, but I really wanted to understand you.

Seriously, I mean it. The first time I saw you, I just knew. We're the same. We had to be friends."

For a minute both of us were quiet.

"What made you think that?" I asked her.

I wasn't trying to sound anything but normal, but my voice was doing things I could not comprehend. It wasn't my voice anymore. I kept wiping my face with my handkerchief.

"Because of how your eyes—"

I spoke up before she could finish.

"Was it my eye, though, or the bullying?"

"Both," she said. "I mean, they can't be separated." Her face was serious. "You've gone through so much because of your eyes. It's a painful thing, I know, but it's also made you who you are. That's for sure. And because I won't give up my signs, I've gone through a lot, too. If we didn't have them, everything would be different. That's why I knew that I would understand you, better than anyone else, and why you would understand the way I feel better than anyone else. I knew it. And I wasn't wrong. When I sent you the letter, you came. You think about how other people feel. You're so kind. It makes sense. Because we're always in pain, we know exactly what it means to hurt somebody else. Maybe it's not as bad for me as it is for you, but I think I know how you feel, probably more than anybody."

Kojima moved from the railing to the stairs and sat on the third step up from the landing. That part of the stairs was always dark. Just seeing Kojima step into the darkness gave me chills. From where I stood in the unforgiving summer sun, I gazed up at Kojima, perched in the shadows. She sat with her elbows on her knees, chin cupped in her hands. Staring down at me.

"I really like your eyes."

She said it slowly, loud and clear.

"No one's ever told me that before," I said. "Ever."

She kept on looking at me.

I felt so at ease that it disturbed me, but I spoke my mind.
I wasn't sure what I was saying. I listened to what I was saying.
This definitely wasn't my voice.

"You don't mind that I'm the first one, do you?"

I nodded vaguely at what she was saying, and didn't stop.
As I nodded, I felt the strength leave my body, draining from
my fingertips. I thought I might need to sit down.

"I know there's so much pain in this, but we have to keep
going. I have my signs because of the way my family is, and you
are who you are because of your eyes. That's why we were able
to meet. That's why we can talk like this, why we can be
together like this. A time will come when everything will be
clear. Even the other kids will understand. A time will come,
I'm sure of it, when everything will be alright."

Kojima stood up and toed her right foot forward. Her face
and her body were still behind the darkness of the stairs, but
the tip of her sneaker poked into the brilliant sunlight. She
came down the stairs toward me. The breeze picked up, and
everything started to glide. Her thick hair floated on the wind,
lifting like a handkerchief made from the softest material imag-
inable.

I realized she was standing right beside me, staring into my
left eye, really close. I looked back into hers. I took off my
glasses so I could bring my eye closer. I realized the blackness
of her pupils was actually a rich array of browns. In the dark-
est part, I saw a quivering point of light, tiny as a pinprick.

For a while we just stood there, not saying anything, staring into each other. Then Kojima, hesitating, took my right hand
into both her hands and stroked my fingers with her fingertips,
and spread my fingers to examine my palm, before squeezing
my hand flat like a pancake. Her fingers and palms were moist
with sweat. Her hands were colder than mine, and so small.
She held my hand and I squeezed hers. This was the first time
I touched Kojima.

The cicadas were lowering their voices, sinking into the distance. I realized I could barely hear them anymore. The roaring heat from earlier had left my skin. Kojima had a look on her face that was nothing like any face I'd ever seen her make before, and it was right next to mine.

Chapter Four

Approaching the first day of September, when school would start again, I felt something happening in my body. Whatever I saw, whatever I thought about, no longer felt real. When I lay awake in bed, my throat stung like it was being speared. A weight pressed on my chest. Sometimes it manifested as a fever. I probably could have used it as an excuse to start school later, but only by a couple of days at most, and my absence may have drawn the attention of Ninomiya and his friends, which was something I was hoping to avoid. The last thing I wanted was to pique their curiosity.

When I was sitting by the door, putting on my shoes to go, my mom wondered out loud if it was a cold.

"Just try to go," she said. "If you feel too crummy, you can always come home."

The summer showed no sign of ending.

It was as if this summer would last all year, until another summer finally took its place. The days retained all of the humidity and heat and brutal sunlight of summer at its peak, refusing to relent.

Nothing had changed at school. The same old crowd of rowdy classmates, up to the same old things. Same uniforms, same color to their skin, same way of slouching in their chairs, and the same tone of voice for all the same topics. The trips they took, or the famous singers they saw. Their voices blended into one voice, the voice of the class.

Between classes, as I was fanning myself with one of my

folders, one of the girls practically spat at me. "Watch yourself, Eyes." Another one said "What, you're still alive?" and laughed. A juice box came at me through the air. Same old thing.

Kojima sat rigid in her seat.

No matter how long I watched that head of hair, it never moved. No one spoke to Kojima, and Kojima spoke to no one. Staring at her back, I imagined myself walking up to her and saying, "Hey Kojima," the way normal people talk. "How was your week?" She'd look at me, raising her eyebrows, then probably giggle. No, definitely. I can see the hair on her lip now, the stains on the neck of her shirt. Those were her signs. They mattered. And there was nothing wrong with them. What if I explained that to the class?

"Hey, everybody. Know the things you always make fun of Kojima for? Guess what? They all serve a purpose. They're her way of remembering the time she spent living with her dad. All of you have things you value more than anything, right? Photos, or maybe letters. In reality, it's all just paper, but we project our memories and emotions onto them, giving them meaning, and that's what makes them more than paper. And out of all those pictures and letters, I bet one or two stand out from the rest, special in a way that no one else would ever understand. That's what it feels like for Kojima to look the way she does. I know it might seem weird, but if photos and letters can mean that much, if you can admit how much they mean to you, is it really so strange that being dirty could do the same thing for someone else? We all see the world in our own way."

At first they would look stunned, or at least pretend to be, but as my explanation sank in, they would sigh to show they understood. Like they knew it was true. Then Kojima would turn around and smile, like she was free and happy, and we could enjoy talking about all the things we did on our own over the summer.

Someone bumped into my desk and roused me from the fantasy. The bell was ringing. Time for class. The teacher walked in wearing an orange polo shirt. His arms and face were burnt to a crisp.

I kept my hands inside the cool space in my desk and half-listened as the teacher spoke. Sometimes he'd say something and the class would kind of laugh. I just watched, barely conscious, but I could see that Kojima was the only one sitting still. She didn't move a muscle. Gazing at her triggered dark emotions. I had zero power. Who was I kidding, less than zero. I could never do any of those things I was imagining. Nothing I could do would actually free Kojima. She was, what, ten feet away? I couldn't even call her name.

I got this letter from Kojima in the last week of September. The tone of the writing was nothing like any other letter she had given me.

> *Greetings and salutations. Can you believe it's still this hot?*
>
> *I'm glad I sit over by the window now. I've been wanting to tell you. So I'm writing you a letter for the first time in a while. I know we see each other at school, but it feels like we haven't talked in forever. How are you? When I'm at home, and when I'm at school, I think a lot about the time over summer when we went to the museum, and what we talked about on the stairs. How about you? I know this is random, but you're so nice. I think so, at least. When I think about it, it almost hurts. I can't put it any better than that. You and I talked about all kinds of things, but I hope we can keep it up, just like in the spring. I really want us to keep talking, and talk about even more things. What about you? Maybe you're thinking, "What's left to talk about?" But, I swear, if we meet up again, we'll have all kinds of things to say. How about we meet on the stairs and talk some more?*

By the way, I wanted to tell you, I finally kind of had a fight with my mom's new guy (although there's nothing new about him, as a human being or in our lives). Well, it wasn't really a fight. Just a tiff. In the heat of the moment, though, I said everything that was on my mind. He had this stupid look on his face, like he knows everything. He was smiling the whole time. I've never been more upset in my whole life. Meanwhile, he heard me out, with that dumb smile, then gave me one of his life lectures and looked really smug about it. I couldn't stop thinking how this guy has probably never had a chance to think about anything that actually matters.

When you think about it that way, it's kind of sad. Like, maybe it's not his fault. I started to think that maybe I should forgive him. I wondered if maybe he's sort of a victim, too. It got me thinking.

Honestly, I started wondering about the other kids at school. Just like we're victims, they could be victims of something bigger than any of us.

I felt sorry for them, when they laughed in my face and called me names or came after me in the bathroom. But if I told them everything I'm telling you, they would never understand. Same way that I learned from what they've done to me, I think they need to learn, but not from me. It has to be a consequence of their own actions. Otherwise, they'll never understand. They need to learn about themselves from what they've done to me. That would be enough to justify my life. Anyway, I could probably write about my thoughts forever, but this letter has gotten pretty long. I think I've been writing for like five hours. I just really wanted to talk. Sorry to go on and on. I should stop here. Bye for now.

She'd never written me anything that long. It took me ten times as long to read it.

I tried writing back, but I couldn't. She had made so many

references to things she had said to me the last time we had seen each other. I understood what she was saying, but I had nothing to share. Shying away from the blank lines on the paper, I thought about Kojima, and thought about myself. After a while, I pulled the slipcase down from my bookshelf and read through all the letters she'd ever written me. They were all so lively, like she was right there next to me, speaking her mind. As I went, I got caught up in wondering about how my letters sounded to her, what kind of mood they conveyed. What had I been writing? I remembered how she wrote once about when you send someone a letter, how it's out of your hands. It's not yours anymore, even though you wrote it.

I stuffed her letters back into the slipcase and lay down on my bed, staring at the ceiling. I wanted to see her so badly.

I sat up, but forced myself back to bed and closed my eyes. Every second, her name strobed through my nervous system, getting larger and larger, filling my blood. I sat up again and pulled down the slipcase and read through those old letters from the beginning. I was unsure of how I felt about the long one or how I should respond. Going through her letters made me sure I wanted to see her, but feeling the way I did, I wondered if I should even write to her at all. I thought about the time she said she liked my eyes. I replayed every second of that minute in my mind. She really liked my eyes. The memory stood on my chest. The pain was good and bad at the same time. I couldn't move. Maybe I wanted something else from her, something more. Something was taking root inside of me, something that letters alone could not sustain. Its roots dug deep. I flipped over onto my stomach and stuffed my face into the pillow, thinking about Kojima in the undulating darkness.

CHAPTER FIVE

At the start of October, my mom's older sister, which I guess made her my step-aunt, passed away, and I went to my first funeral.

This step-aunt, whom I had never met, was older than my mom by seven years, unmarried with no kids.

My dad couldn't come because of work, so I wound up going with my mom. I didn't know the first thing about this person. My dad told me I didn't have to go, but I felt like my mom would be sad if she had to go on her own. When I told her I would go with her, she warned me it was far, but she also seemed sort of relieved.

The funeral was a quiet affair. A dozen or so relatives gathered in the function room of a community center. We sat on our heels with our heads down while the incense burned and a monk chanted the sutras, ending each passage with a bell, clicking through his string of prayer beads. My turn came to burn a stick of incense. Every now and then, I heard a few people sobbing. I kept my face down, staring at my knees the whole time.

When the service was over, it was time to say goodbye, and everyone put flowers in the casket. I looked inside. Her lips were parted, and she had white cotton stuffed up her nose. Her face was nondescript, but I couldn't really tell if this was because she was dead, or because she was born like that. Seeing my first dead body, I felt something like horror, or maybe disgust, but while I didn't want to take another step, I knew I had to see what made this different from a living body, and couldn't bring myself to look away.

I tried to take a moment of reflection, but clearly I had nothing to reflect upon. It helped ground me to remember I was seeing off a stranger, who had almost no relationship to me. That much was a relief.

After the coffin was taken away, the relatives set up for lunch. Mom didn't want to stay, so we went home. No crematorium for us. Her relatives couldn't keep their eyes off me, but whenever I looked back, they turned away. When a few people said hi to my mom, she introduced me. No one was anything less than polite. I didn't ask who anybody was, and she didn't bother telling me. I saw her mother, or my step-grandma or whatever. I knew her as soon as I spotted her, but she didn't say anything to Mom after the ceremony, and of course she said nothing to me. We left before they handed out the bento boxes.

"We need salt," Mom said. We were on the train home. "To sprinkle before going in the house."

"What for?"

"Purification."

Mom and I sat quietly on the swaying train. She looked really tired. But aside from that, and the fact that we were on our way home from a funeral, it was a gorgeous afternoon. Waiting for the train, I fixated on the face that I had seen inside the coffin, imagining its skin, its complexion, all the wrinkles, but when the train pushed off I forgot everything. The wobbling train made me think about Kojima. The sunlight streaming in and the scenery we passed were totally different, but for an instant, I was back inside that train, barreling ahead into summer. I remembered every word she said when she was on the bench beside me.

"That was weird, right?" my mom asked out of nowhere.

Her voice snapped me back into reality. I waited for her to go on, but she didn't say anything else.

"What was?" I finally asked.

"I don't know," she said. "The whole day, I guess."

"Was it?"

"Very," she said. "It really drained me."

Mom was quiet after that. She closed her eyes and didn't move.

We got off at our station and stopped at the supermarket on the way home. As we went through the store, the other customers eyed my mom in her funeral clothes and me in my uniform. Mom didn't pay them any mind and filled a basket with spinach and onions and sliced pork. I asked if it was okay for us to be inside before we did the salt thing, and she said the supermarket was strong enough to take it. I carried both bags of groceries. When we were back at our apartment building, waiting for the elevator, she thanked me for coming, without looking right at me. I told her I'd be happy to go next time. She sighed and gave me a hug. She looked confused, but smiled for my sake.

The trip out to the funeral and back wiped me out. I was exhausted and had to stay home from school for three days. I kept thinking about how nice it would be if I could stay home forever, but I knew there was no way.

Four days after the funeral, I left the house early as usual and took the tree-lined street to school. The bed of earth stretching between the trees had turned rich brown with moisture. I took a deep breath through my nose, but the smell of rain was gone. All the same, the soil was moist and slurped with every step, threatening to suck my shoes into the earth.

It must have rained at some point during the night. No one else was on the path. I heard an engine revving far away. I trudged toward school as if I were dragging the entire street behind me.

There was no one standing at the entrance. There never was

this early. The gate had been left open, but only slightly. I walked across the schoolyard to the building in the back. No one but me. Halfway across, I looked up at the building I was passing. It stood there like the weathered bones of some enormous creature. The platform in the middle of the field was crooked, with flaking paint, like some partially digested section of the skeleton.

I entered the classroom and sat down at my desk. When I pulled it closer, something felt different about the way it moved. I went to put my hands inside, but touched what felt like a torn strip of fabric. I crouched down to investigate and realized the whole desk was stuffed with junk. I tugged on the fabric, and a heavy bundle flopped onto the floor, where it unraveled on its own.

Bread crusts stale as paper dipped in cornstarch, and what looked like maggots . . . but were actually little beads of dried-up tangerine, mixed in with bunched-up gym clothes and school slippers, which I recognized as mine, together with some keys, a weird stuffed animal, a face mask, a stack of handouts, potatoes that were growing eyes, library books, a scrub brush, the chalkboard eraser, and a pack of strawberry milk that must have been half-full, since it was dribbling from the straw. The smell was awful. I tilted the desk and looked inside. There was more. A black plastic bag spilling used pads and tampons.

I stood there looking at what had come out of my desk. Then I sat in my chair and stared at the mess by my feet. You would have thought I knew what my own seat would feel like, but the backrest and the metal parts dug into my skin. I couldn't find a way to sit that felt okay.

I don't know how long I spent gawking at the junk around me, but at some point I heard someone coming down the hall. For some reason, I thought it was that girl from the last day before summer and held my breath. As the footsteps drew closer, my heart sped up, and I remembered the shape of her uniform and how straight her bangs were, and the face Momose had been making. I went tense. But it was a different girl. She looked at my desk and immediately looked away, put down her bag and left the room. This girl always came after me during roll call. I didn't move after she left. According to the clock above the blackboard, it would probably be ten minutes until everyone showed up. I got up and grabbed a plastic bag from the cleaning supply locker right by the door and picked up all the stuff from around my desk.

Ninomiya's friends showed up with the crowd of other kids. One guy knocked me in the head with his folder. They had a good laugh and asked me why I smelled so bad.

"Hey Eyes, what happened to your desk?" one of them asked, still laughing. I sat motionless and didn't answer.

"We heard someone in your family died." It was the guy who hit me with his folder. "We offer our, uh, what was it called again?" he asked another student next to him.

"It's eulogy."

"No, elegy."

They were having a great time. The word they were groping for was "condolences," but I wasn't going to be the one to say it.

Ninomiya, who had been making some girls laugh a few desks away, came over to join us. When he got near me he pinched his nose and moaned like he was puking.

"What is that? What the hell is that smell?" He waved his hand in front of his face. "You trying to kill us or something? Wash yourself before you come to class. You ever take a bath?"

Everyone thought this was hilarious.

"And I thought that Kojima girl was supposed to be the nasty one," someone added.

I froze at the mention of Kojima. It felt like I was hugging a ball of ice.

"One's enough for one class," Ninomiya said, arms crossed. "Two's a biohazard."

He looked at me like he was sizing me up.

"You've got two options. Get naked and wash yourself off in the fountain, right now, or we're going to play a little game after school. Your call."

I sat there in my chair, not saying anything.

"No answer means you choose the game."

I didn't answer.

"Game it is. Can't wait. I found this in a book while you were gone. You're gonna love it."

He laughed. So did everybody else.

"Don't leave," he said. "You do, you're dead."

I stared in silence at the surface of my desk.

White words spread across the blackboard, only to vanish. Why should I come to school if it meant going through all this? No matter how many times I asked the question, there would never be an answer.

But if I wanted to stop going to school, if I really had to stop, I would need to give my mom a reason.

I had imagined sitting my mom down and telling her, but I could never follow through. I didn't want her to know about me being bullied. And I definitely didn't want my father to find out, no matter what. If he did, I can't even imagine what would happen. I knew that if I told them the truth, neither of them would want anything to do with me. If they found out I was being bullied, I was good as dead.

I thought about dropping out, but I wasn't sure how that worked. Everyone has to finish middle school. It's the law. Was quitting even possible? Even if I got my mom to let me leave, what was I supposed to do with the rest of my life? This line of thinking never ended well. If I never finished middle school, I wouldn't be allowed into high school, but I had no idea how

I could survive another year of this. If I could get some kind of job, I could get through however many decades I had left. But who would hire me? Which leads to where I always wound up when I thought this way. Say I dropped out for a while, but somehow got my act together and finished my diploma and even college. It would probably seem like I was in the clear. But there was no guarantee I would be safe for good. None whatsoever. As long as I looked like I did, with this eye, I would always be a target. What if they were waiting, ready to ambush me wherever I went next? A hideous fate hiding down the road, waiting for me to pass.

The day was ending, and then it was over. I was so agitated by my fear I couldn't sit still.

I waited for the moment when everybody got up to leave. When Ninomiya and his friends weren't looking, I grabbed my bag and eased into the flow of bodies exiting the classroom. My stomach made a fist. I wondered if it was what I had for lunch, but I couldn't remember eating lunch. I fell into the ranks of students heading for their clubs, pushing through the crush of gossip. My sole objective was escape. I had no time to consider what I was going to do afterward, much less tomorrow.

Rounding a corner with my eyes down, I almost collided with Kojima.

She looked scared and took a step back, but then she saw it was me. She drew her lips tight and smiled at me, but only with her eyes. I was breathing so hard that I could hear all of the air come out of me. A wet heat pulsed around my eyes.

Kojima was carrying a dinged-up trash can that looked like a little oil drum. She was always the one who had to take the trash out. With the flat of her other hand, she rubbed her stomach.

"Kojima."

I said it. Loud and clear.

The first time I had ever said her name at school.

None of the other students walking through the hall noticed. Kojima set the trash bin on the floor of the hall, hesitant to let it go. She was conscious of the kids around us, but she took a good long look at me. I took a deep breath and said her name again. Kojima. And said it again. She frowned like she was asking what was wrong, but between the moments when she looked down or turned to see who else was coming, she looked me in the eye.

"Sorry I couldn't answer," I said, licking my lips and wringing out the words. "I've been thinking a lot and . . ."

But Kojima's eyes jumped to something behind me. A dull pain plowed into my leg. On the way down, I did my best to dodge Kojima, twisting away from her, but landed on my shoulder and bashed my cheekbone on the floor.

Ninomiya was standing next to the guy who had kicked me. He didn't look amused.

"Where do you think you're going?"

They marched me across the school, through the courtyard, to the area in front of the gymnasium.

This place was usually packed with teams doing stretches or waving their rackets, or kids whose clubs needed to use the gym, but there was not a kid in sight. The going-home music played like a lullaby from the speakers on the poles, and in the distance you could just make out the voices of girls screeching at each other, having fun, calling each other's names.

I was wondering where everybody was, but then it hit me. Once a month, to accommodate the faculty meeting, all clubs and extracurricular activities were cancelled, and all students, without exception, were supposed to leave the school as soon as classes were over.

The front door to the gymnasium was locked. No surprise. We went around to the left and skirted the sheer face of the building, stopping at a low door. It was marked as an emergency exit, made from what looked to be flimsy aluminum. They turned the knob and went in, shoes on, pushing at the shoulders of my blazer. From where the door opened, it was a few steps up to a wing of the stage at the back of the gymnasium, where the bundled curtains dangled from the ceiling. The old fabric stank of dust. When I stopped, they shoved me from behind so hard I tripped and almost fell over. My bag slipped off my shoulder, and the book in the open front pocket fell to my feet. I hurried to stuff it back in.

I had been in the gymnasium countless times, for assemblies and for gym class, but now it looked like somewhere I had never been. The ceiling was far, far taller than I had ever realized, and the space was truly cavernous.

The guys were hyper. Once we were in, they started bouncing around. One kid whooped and Ninomiya told him to shut up. After that, something happened to the way their footsteps, and their quiet voices and their stifled laughter echoed. Sound took on a weird weight, like it was fatter. When it hit the walls, it ricocheted.

We heard something by the emergency exit. Everybody shut up and looked, but it was just Momose.

From where I stood, I could see him step inside and close the door, and hear the metal clink when he locked it a second later.

When Ninomiya saw Momose, his face eased into a grin, and he shot him a wave. Barely reacting, Momose strode over to us with his hands stuffed in his blazer pockets. I thought I heard him whistle, but I could have been imagining things. He seemed to catch a glimpse of me, but this, too, could have been my mind playing tricks. Entering his field of vision didn't guarantee that he noticed I was there. His eyes were open, but they held no agitation or emotion. Counting him and Ninomiya, there were six of them.

Ninomiya walked over to the front entrance, where the thick curtains had been drawn so that you couldn't see inside. He reached behind a pile of mats and fished around for something. When he found what looked like a mask, he came back toward us with it in his hands.

"Put this on," he said, holding up some kind of a deflated ball. It had a gash across the face. "We're gonna play soccer—or something like it."

It was a volleyball. I felt myself shaking my head.

"Truth is, I wanted a real soccer ball, but there weren't any." He spun the puckered volleyball in his hands. "Obviously, right? You're not supposed to play soccer in here."

Ninomiya snorted.

"Soccer balls are way more expensive than volleyballs. They put numbers on all of them. After practice, if they're even one ball short, they'll keep searching until it turns up. If they can't find it, all the first-year kids get punished."

He stuck a finger in the slit cut in the ball and turned it inside out, rolling back the skin.

"I can be real sweet, you know. That's why you get a volleyball. They're not as easy to find as ping pong balls, but they had plenty to spare. Besides, the volleyball is definitely my favorite of all balls. It's got a good texture. Nice and soft against your skin, like a bandage . . ."

I stared at Ninomiya's feet.

"I read this book over vacation. I don't know what came over me. Not like I'm into reading. But sometimes I figure what the hell. Anyway, I read the whole thing. What about you? I bet you're a big reader."

He was asking me.

"You dropped that book earlier. What was it? Any good?"

I couldn't give him an answer.

"I don't get novels. Reading about other people's lives or whatever. Who cares? I mean, you have your own life, don't you?

You'd see it if you ever put the book down. Why go out of the way to get caught up in someone else's made-up life?"

I was still unable to answer.

"It's just like magic. Not real magic. Bogus magic. What's there to like? It's a gimmick. A trick. In reality, nothing's gonna change. No, maybe reading does change things. It makes them worse. Ruins your day. Anyway, it's just a load of bull. If it's not real magic, what's the point? It's just boring."

Ninomiya told me to take off my tie, then reconsidered and told me I should lose my glasses too. He had one of his guys take them off my face and bind my hands behind my back using the tie.

"Not too tight," he said and laughed. Momose stood a few paces away with his arms crossed, gazing toward me as he traced his left pointer finger across his lip.

"Human soccer," Ninomiya said. "I know that it's a volley-ball, but you get the point. We're gonna be kicking, so it's closer to soccer than volleyball. The first one to get you into the goal wins."

He looked at the other guys.

"We're playing one-on-one, elimination. You two go first, then you guys, then me and Momose. Winner moves on."

He clapped his hands.

"Alright," he said. "Shoes off. Set up the goals."

A couple of the guys walked to opposite sides of the court, took off their shoes, and set them down six feet apart from each other, creating a pair of makeshift goals.

I twisted my wrists but my hands weren't coming free. What could I do if they did? They would just tie me up again, only tighter. Sweat was dripping from my armpits and down my back, even down my thighs.

"Eyes, I want you to be the best ball you can be. Be one with the ball. Know what I mean? You better move like a real ball."

Ninomiya stretched at the gash in the distended volleyball

and fitted it around my scalp. He yanked down hard, but couldn't pull the skin down past my temples. It wasn't going to fit.

"Your ears are huge," he said. "Man, this is pissing me off."

Momose came over. Without a word, he grabbed the ball and ripped open the gash before stretching it back over my head. It squeaked as he fitted it around my skull, until the moment when my nose filled with the smell of dust and I could no longer see. My body cramped into a tight mass, and I could see a psychotic animation flashing just behind my forehead. I shook my head like a maniac and tried to run, but one of them kicked me in the leg and yelled at me to stand still. The skin of the ball stopped before my chin, leaving my bottom lip open to the air.

"Volleyballs are way smaller than they look," Ninomiya said, as if genuinely surprised. "Alright. Let's do this."

Ensconced in a darkness whose color I could not define, and unable to allow myself to stand, I spun and writhed, searching for a defense. I had no clue what my body was doing. A tepid lava, black and leaden, rose over my ankles and climbed my legs. It probed my mouth and pumped into my lungs. In no time, it was melting me, working from the inside. I moved my legs, trying to escape, but lost my balance and fell flat. Back on my knees, I tried to stand, but they knocked me down onto my back. Wading through their choked laughter and their breathing, I did the same things over and over and was knocked down every time.

"You're not the best ball I've ever seen," said Ninomiya, "but you'll do."

One of them grabbed me by the arms and hoisted me up, dragging me as I kicked. They yelled at me to stand up straight.

"Come on, let's do this. When I say go. Just like soccer, alright? Proper kicks, boys."

My clasped hands were white at the knuckles, and my knees

were quivering so badly that I could almost hear them vibrate. I flexed every single muscle, squeezed my eyes shut, and clenched my teeth so hard I felt the blood pulse through my forehead. My face was hideous. I felt my lips retreating from my teeth. Breath bubbled through my spit. I had never felt my heart beat so ferociously. My pulse crunched in my ear, like wet sand. Like if I stuck my finger in, I could have felt it. This was the first time I experienced panic as a sound.

"Game on," Ninomiya said.

The air shifted around us. An instant later, the sky cracked open, a shockwave burst into infinity, and a silver light flashed before my eyes like a rogue flame. I had no idea what happened. I felt my legs swing through the air. With all my weight, I slammed back-first into the floor. I couldn't breathe. Pain spiraled from the center of my face, and my mind scurried through consciousness. The pain was accompanied by a discernible sound, but I had no way of knowing if the sound was real, or even what it sounded like, no matter how close I listened. My entire face grew numb, like a section of it had been blown away. On the floor, I rounded my back as best I could to scrunch into a ball and brought my face into my knees, while rings of hot pain radiated from my head.

I had no idea how much time had passed before Ninomiya spoke. He sounded annoyed at one of the guys, and the others echoed his displeasure.

"Hey, slow down. Have some respect. I want a clean game."

Tears were streaming down my face. Floodgates open. My whole face was wet. The endless tears soaked my lips and dripped down my chin. I felt it spreading from my temple, pressed against the floor, into my scalp.

I couldn't move. Someone's hands grabbed my head and tugged. My face came free from the ball. It was painfully bright, even with my eyes shut. I couldn't open them or sit up.

I still couldn't feel my face. Tears gushed from my eyes

nonstop. After a while, I felt them loosening the necktie they had tied around my hands, and saw through squinting eyes the silhouette of legs. They kicked over my glasses. When I reached out a hand and grabbed for them, I noticed the blood pooling on the floor. Like someone had left a sink running, only blood. Fresh blood, primary red. I opened my eyes wide, amazed I had had this much blood to lose. I grabbed my glasses and pulled the tip of my finger through the blood. It had a slickness different from the tears. I brought my finger under my left eye. The blood was so wet and slimy that I thought it would start talking to me any second.

I couldn't tell whether the blood was coming from a cut in my head or bleeding from my nose, but the numbness around my nose showed no sign of stopping.

"Game over," Ninomiya said languidly and clapped once.

The antsy whispering around him paused, until somebody yawned, and they began to talk again in quiet voices.

"No more human soccer," said Ninomiya, not even remotely fazed. "You ruined it."

I sat up with the help of my hands and knees and touched gently for my nose. It was still there, but the contact of my fingers made it roar. I swallowed the pain and put on my glasses. The feeling of the bridge resting on my face nearly made me lose my breath. I opened my spasming eyes and blinked wide. I blinked and blinked.

Ninomiya was staring down at me. Momose stood behind him with his arms crossed, with all his weight on one leg. It seemed like he was looking at me too. It sounded like the other guys were screwing around. Intermittently, I heard their sneakers squeak against the floor as they tried, and failed, to keep from laughing.

"Eyes, don't let anybody see you on the way home. We're out of here. You wait here thirty minutes, got it? Thirty minutes. The faculty meeting probably won't be over yet, but you still need to be careful. I know I don't have to tell you this, but you better not tell anybody about this. That goes double for your family. Wait, hold on."

He gave himself a chance to think.

"Listen," he said. "In thirty minutes, go out the way we came in and head over to the AV room. Behind it, there's a part of the wall that's lower than the rest. Climb over that and get the hell out of here. We got to be sure. You can hop it if you actually try. Not like you have a choice. Okay?"

I was sitting up, but hung my head, watching the pool of blood before me. The blood staining the chest of my shirt was just as red, and I couldn't tell you what color the blood on my blazer was. The guys all shuffled toward the door, but Ninomiya turned around, like he remembered something.

"Clean yourself up before you leave," he said, but pointed at the door and shook his head. "No using the water outside. Use the tap over there. Get cleaned up, then beat it."

After they shut the door behind them, I lay back down and let go of my mind, staring up at the ceiling.

It was useless to try to think.

All I could do was open my mouth wide, to breathe air in and out. As I lay breathing, my bleeding body rose up to the ceiling, joining the gridlike pattern of the rafters.

The me at the ceiling turned to face the me lying on my back on the floor, and only then began to descend. I was wearing my uniform and glasses and was bloody from the eyes down; I was getting closer by the second. When we were only six feet apart, he halted in midair.

The me who was floating motionless just stared at me, not saying anything. His eyes were thick like gelatin behind his glasses, directionless as far as I could tell. I muttered to him. What do you think you're looking at?

Facing me like this, I saw how small I was. Wrists and ankles and neck laughably thin, not a hint of strength. My blazer didn't fit well in the shoulders, and my shirt, crimson at the chest, had come untucked. My pants were at least a size too big. I looked like my body had been tacked to the sky at a precarious angle.

I had been gazing up for some time at my body stuck there in the air, when my lips on the me above me parted. I realized I was saying something, but the motion was so subtle that I was unable to read my lips. Some moments later, the me above me relaxed his face. I had the feeling he was smiling at me. It really looked like this blood-drenched version of me overhead was smiling. I couldn't understand what this was supposed to mean, but I lay there staring back into my face. When I sniffed, vast quantities of phlegm came down into my mouth and gathered on my tongue. I hesitated for a second, but tilted my head to the side and spat it out. I spat blood mixed with phlegm and tiny bubbles. There were little bits of black inside it too.

I heard the sound of the door opening and froze. A teacher must have heard us and came to check things out.

But it was Kojima.

She stood by the door, looking over at me. Then, as if something had unpaused her, she ran to where I was.

She knelt on the floor and looked me over, scowling.

"There's blood everywhere," she said. "Does it hurt?" She shook her head and licked her lips, like she was going to do something.

"Yeah," I said, "but it's over now."

"I followed them here and came in when I saw them leave." Her voice shook as if a powerful wind were blowing through it.

"Sorry, I'm freaking out . . . can you get up?" She reached out to touch my shoulders. She kept nodding at me and swallowing her spit. You could hear it.

"I think so," I said. "I've never seen this much blood."

I tried to smile and wiped the back of my hand under my nose to have a look. There was still gooey blood there, but the blood in my nostrils was beginning to clot. The throbbing sensation had gotten worse, like electricity was hugging my face. Kojima sat down on the floor beside me.

Finally I sat up and tucked my shirt into my pants. I found my tie and stuffed it in my blazer pocket.

I made my way over to the sink that Ninomiya had been pointing at. When I stood up, my head was spinning, but I managed to walk in a straight line. My face smarted with every step.

The white porcelain sink had a large crack in it. Beside it was a bucket with a stiff rag inside and a long-handled mop, with a head as stiff as the rag. I turned on the faucet and let out a cool trickle of water. I cupped it in my hands and splashed my face, doing my best to wash it. When my hands touched skin, the pain became concentrated. It felt like my face was going to split open. The rag had been wrung into a wad and left that way. I dropped it into a bucketful of water and carried it to where the blood was. Then Kojima went to the sink and found another rag so she could help. We sopped up the blood without talking. Wiping added water to the mix, diluting the blood, giving us more work. Kojima wrung her rag dry and wiped the floor. Where the blood had started to dry, I dug in with my fingernails. The water in the bucket was clouded with dirt from the rags and the thinning blood. Soon we couldn't see the bottom.

"I was watching from over there, through the window."

Kojima's voice was quiet. She scrubbed and stared at the floor. I wiped the floor and nodded.

"I watched until they started kicking. Then I started shaking. I couldn't take it."

"Yeah." I nodded again and twisted my rag over the bucket.

"They've done it to me, too," she said. "In the bathroom. Punched me to the ground and stuff." Now she was even quieter. "I didn't bleed, but it really hurt. They're always careful to make sure nobody notices. They're good at covering their tracks. Scary good. Where do you think they learn that?"

"There's got to be some book or something that breaks it down," I said, not looking at Kojima, "point by point, how to get away with it."

"You think they read about it, then try it out on us?" Kojima almost whispered.

I didn't answer.

"Do you think we're practice?" she asked. "Or are we the real thing?"

Probably both, I thought. I rinsed out my rag in a clean bucket of water and squeezed it dry before wiping up whatever was left. When we were done, I stood up and had a look at the floor. The blood was gone without a trace.

"What are you going to do about your clothes?" she asked, looking at my face.

Kojima looked exhausted. I had lost track of how long we had been wiping the floor. I wondered how long I had been in the gymnasium. I gazed up at the windows by the catwalk encircling the enormous room, to check the color of the sky, but it was colorless and told me nothing. It looked at once as if nothing had changed from when we got here, and yet as if the day were on the verge of ending. Without looking at her face, I thanked Kojima for helping me. She stared right at me. I felt her staring at my nose and mouth. I can't even imagine what she saw.

"You don't need to thank me. But what are you going to do about your clothes?" she asked again.

"I'll figure it out," I said, "it'll be okay."

Kojima and I stepped out through the emergency exit and closed the door behind us. Making sure the coast was clear, we jogged toward the rear of the nearest building. The narrow space between the school building and the stone wall bordering the grounds was secluded in shadow and overgrown with mossy weeds, with empty cans and work gloves littering the edges. Following the building, we came upon the section of wall Ninomiya must have been talking about. Tall, but shorter than the rest.

"Why did we come this way?" Kojima asked, a few steps behind me.

"I have to go this way," I said after a pause, staring at the wall. "There's blood on my clothes, and I can't let anybody see me leave through the main gate."

Somehow this justification sapped the energy from my arms and legs. The sensation made me question who this defense was meant for and what purpose it served.

"What's on the other side of the wall?" she asked.

"I don't know," I said. "I've never done this before, but since the main gate is over there, it's got to lead behind the school." I had no clue what I was saying but my lips moved anyway. "You don't think I should go this way?"

"No, you should go out the front, like normal. It won't be a problem if anyone sees you. Just say you stayed behind to do something in class."

Kojima and I both stood there for a minute, not saying anything.

It hurt to have Kojima see me looking so pathetic. I wanted to disappear. I stood there, waiting for her to leave. But she didn't budge, just stood there staring at my back.

"Hey," she finally said, "I'll leave after you make it over."

I wanted to tell her I would rather she left now, but I couldn't say the words. I stood in silence with my back to her.

"Does it hurt?" she asked me, sounding a little worried.

I didn't say anything.

"I think you need to go to a hospital," she said. "I'm serious."

"Okay, I will."

"Good."

"See you," I said.

I reached up to grab the top of the stone wall. It was short enough that I didn't need to stretch. My body felt dull and heavy, like lead baked into clay. None of my muscles felt even remotely muscular, and once I had a foot pressed into the low part of the wall, I wasn't sure what to do next. I just wanted to disappear.

My fingers on the wall were screaming. Although I understood the necessary steps for going up and over, the next move was beyond me. I scrambled and fell, feet flat on the earth. Kojima stood behind me, holding my bag. My face throbbed. Speechless, I grabbed again and again for the rim of the wall, employing my arms and legs to no avail, failing every time. I could feel a heat rising from my stomach. It reached my face, but it had nowhere to go. When I breathed through my nose, shreds of clotted blood pressed against my sinuses and caused the pain to splinter. I couldn't turn around and see Kojima's face. I wanted to be out of sight already. The soles of my sneakers scraped against the straight face of the wall, making a dry sound and kicking up gray dust. But every time I tried, my feet landed in the weedy darkness of the earth.

"Hey," Kojima called to me. I was reaching up to grab the top of the wall.

"Hey," she said again, but this time grabbed my arm and tugged it to pull my body toward her. She was frowning at me, staring at my face.

"Can we talk for a second?"

Her voice was even lower than usual. I cast my eyes down at her feet and said nothing. The laces of her dirty sneakers touched the ground. They were coming untied.

"Watching them gang up on you like that, I felt like I saw something else, something you couldn't see."

She spoke slowly.

"I think you're right," she said. "I mean, we're the same age as them. Our bodies are as big as theirs, and if we wanted to, we could push back. Give them a taste of their own medicine.

We could put up a fight. We could get revenge. But we don't. What's stopping us?"

"I'm too weak to fight back," I answered, but Kojima wasn't buying it.

"That's not why we let them do this," she said. "It's not because we're weak. We're not just following orders or whatever. Maybe it began that way, I don't know. But we're not just obeying, not anymore. We're letting it happen. We know exactly what's going on. We see it, and we let it happen. I don't think that's weakness at all. It's more like strength."

"We let it happen?" I repeated what she said, but I was really asking.

"Yeah. Maybe it looks like they're doing everything while we sit there doing nothing, but that's not true. What we're doing has meaning."

I stood there considering what she was saying.

"Maybe you're right," she said. "Maybe we are weak, in a way. But that's not a bad thing. If we're weak, our weakness has real meaning. We may be weak, but we get it. We know what's important, and we know what's wrong. That's just not true for anyone else in class. They pretend they don't know what's going on. They act nice to the ones who step all over us just to stay on their good side, and to make sure the same thing doesn't happen to them. They act like their hands are clean, but they aren't. They don't get it, not at all. They're no different from the ones who hurt us. The only ones who aren't involved with them are you and me. Like what they did to you in the gym . . . no, what they're always doing, because it's been like this forever. Whatever they do to you, you let it happen. But watching it happen, it was like I saw a crazy knot being undone. Like, everything suddenly made sense. Know what I mean? I think the way you reacted to the situation was right, the only right way to act."

"But what way am I acting?"

I spoke like each word was a flashcard I was pasting onto the space before my eyes.

"I'm just saying, I think you're right." Kojima was crying. "I'm saying you're right."

"Don't cry," I said, facing her. Between the fingers covering her face, I could see her mouth was drawn, hinting at her teeth. Under her palms, her cheeks were blushing. I remembered that first day of summer, on the bench in front of the museum, the first time I had seen Kojima cry. She had cried without moving an inch or making a sound. I had wanted to say something, or knew I had to say something, but seeing her cry like that I failed, as I was failing now, to offer anything of substance.

"Kojima, don't cry," I said softly.

"I'm not," she said.

She looked up and rubbed at her eyes with the backs of her hands.

"I mean, I am. But it's not because I'm sad."

She sniffled and looked into my eyes. That's when she smiled.

"This is proof," she said. "Proof of being right. See? I'm not sad."

I nodded. Kojima took a deep breath, looked up at me, and let out a heavy sigh.

"Do you believe me? About you being right? That's how I feel, with all of my heart. You believe me?"

"I believe you."

". . . the other kids, they're scared of your eyes."

Kojima spoke to me in a small but strong voice, aimed right at me.

"When they say that they're grossed out, they're lying. They're just scared. They're terrified. I don't mean they're scared of the way your eyes look or anything. They're scared to admit there's anything they don't understand. They can't do anything on their own, so they band together, but they aren't really friends, and when something in the world stands out, they get scared and try to destroy it. They try to get rid of it. In reality, they're as scared as anyone, but they trick themselves out of it. They're trying to find peace, but the more they hide, the more numb they become. But that feeling of fear, it stays with them, so it goes on and on, day after day. No matter how they torture us, we never say anything. Especially not to our teachers or our parents. And no matter what they do, we come to school each day, which makes them even more scared. If we ever started screaming or threw ourselves at their feet and started begging, I bet we could make them stop. But we're not just playing by their rules. This is our will. We let them do this. It's almost like we chose this. That's all the more reason why they can't leave us alone. They're so scared, so terrified, and there's nothing they can do to stop it."

When she was finished, Kojima brushed a fingertip over her lips. Then, as if feeling out the contour of her eyeball, she pressed down softly on her right eye. In the changing light, I could make out the tracks of her tears. She looked at me and smiled.

"They'll understand, eventually."

Standing with my feet planted in the darkness, it felt like I could see the air cooling, from the ground up, before my eyes. I was only now realizing that patches of the sky were blocked out by mounds of black clouds, and in the distance I heard the start of thunder. I had no clue what time it was. It hurt to breathe through my nose because it cracked the clotting blood, but I could still smell all kinds of things mixing together with every mouthful of air. I couldn't explain all the different smells, but I felt like I knew them well.

"I really like your eyes," Kojima said. "I said it before, but they're a sign. They matter. Your eyes are who you are."

She looked at me with eyes that could have started crying even now, but she was grinning.

"I really like them."

That night, I could barely sleep.

My body was so heavy and ragged. I kept feeling like I had to throw up, but closing my eyes only stirred my nerves. The darkness behind my eyes drifted between deep and shallow, but it felt like sleep was never going to come. My throat hurt like I was being strangled, and my futon was stiflingly hot. It hurt to breathe. My attempts at sleep just scared sleep away.

I had told my mom a bike ran into me when I wasn't looking. She was stunned when she saw the bloodstains on my shirt. When I said that I had only had a bloody nose, she looked skeptical, but she decided to believe me. After checking me for cuts and bruises, she said I could have hit my head and should probably go to the hospital. I said sure. Talking made my nose throb every time. If it had been broken, it would have hurt much worse. The pain was nothing compared to how it felt after it happened. I'll try sleeping it off first, I said, and went up to my room. I didn't want to talk anymore. Not to her, not to anybody.

I changed out of my bloodstained shirt and went to throw it in the laundry, but my mom said to toss it, so I handed it over without protest. Grimacing, she balled up the shirt and asked me what happened to the other guy. I said he rode away. She asked me what he looked like. I told her it was just some guy. I had been running into people since I was a kid. Bikes had actually run into me before, and I had fallen on my face. All because of my faulty depth perception.

"At least it was a bike," she said and sighed. "What if it had been a car?"

I said I would have bled more—and maybe even died.

The next morning, Mom told me to go to the hospital before school, but I convinced her to let me go on the way home and left for school at the usual time. When I was getting out of bed, there was a new pain in my throat and chest. I had to sit still for a while.

I thought about how nice it would be if I could tell her everything, or better yet, say nothing, and stay in this room forever. But I couldn't stay. Kojima needed me, and I needed her. It's not like we were ever really together at school, but I could remember countless times where it had helped me just to see her from behind and know that she was there. And on the off-chance that it helped Kojima in the same way to have me there, I couldn't just leave her alone in the classroom.

As I walked to school, I tried my best to accurately and thoroughly recall what Kojima had been telling me the day before.

She cried and laughed and told me that she really liked my eyes. It wasn't the first time she said she liked them, but those words had a gentle power that was able to renew me. I had lost sight of what those words could do, but they took me back to where I was before I had the crap kicked out of me.

Kojima said everyone was just scared of my eyes. She said that when they looked at them, and couldn't tell where I was looking, it sent a signal to their brains that there were things they didn't understand, and to keep the scary feeling away, they had to keep on bullying us. She said my eyes are who I am, and that she and I weren't simply giving in, but had chosen things to be this way, and were letting them happen. She said we were letting it happen. That no matter how bad things got, we could never tell on them, and should always come to school, and when it happened all over again, we would take it—that was what really mattered, what had real meaning.

I knew I had to find a way, in my own words, to think about Kojima and me, and what had happened yesterday, and everything before and after that, but first I had to locate the crux of the problem. Was it bullying? At this point, everything was bullying. That didn't help. Was it my lazy eye? Or Kojima's signs? I felt like I had fallen, with my eyes shut, deep into mud that

was not hot or cold. A place unreachable by the solace I absorbed like light when I read Kojima's letters, or met up with her, or even thought of her.

With a loose grip on my thoughts, I continued up the street of trees. At the very middle, I stopped for a second and tried breathing in, inhaling so deeply that I could feel the pain awaken in my lungs. Then I looked up at the sky. Thin watery blue and nothing else. The countless leaves shook in one motion, like a heavy sheet of batting. So heavy I was sure that it would crash down through the branches any minute, engulfing me without apology, before I had a chance to exhale. Whatever had been left of summer had disappeared; I was standing in the thick of autumn, and the light and the soil and the smells had been replenished with its cold, as if a silent rain had fallen when nobody was looking, chilling everything.

My teacher called me to his desk when homeroom was over. He looked horrified.

"What happened to your face?"

"I got hit by a bike," I said.

Today he was wearing a white polo shirt and scratching at the rim of his nostril with the stiff end of a rolled-up handout. He gawked at me.

"When? Yesterday?"

"Yeah."

"On the way home?"

I nodded. After that he asked me when and where it happened, and how they hit me, and what the other guy did after, but I just told him the exact same story I had told my mom.

"I know you can't control an accident, but you can try to be more careful. It looks pretty bad. Did you go to the doctor?"

"Not yet."

"You probably should. It's really swollen. Go see what the nurse says."

He shook his arm to make his watch slip back down to his wrist and raised his voice to tell the class that he had forgotten to tell us that we had health today instead of gym, so come back after lunch. Ninomiya's friends came over to my desk and asked me what I had been saying to the teacher. They laughed, trying to frighten me. I told them exactly what I had told the teacher, and said that that was it. I could tell Kojima was worried, from the way she kept on looking over at me, but I couldn't let them see me looking at her.

I hadn't once seen my own face after the beating. Honestly, it had been forever since the last time I looked into a mirror. At school, I instinctively avoided mirrors in the bathroom and at home, I did my best. It isn't as hard as it might sound. Pretty soon I got used to living without mirrors.

After school, I stopped at home before heading to the local hospital.

Stepping into a world of hospital smells, I saw all kinds of people. A guy with a white bandage wrapped around his head was at the payphone. Most of the people sitting on the benches in front of the huge television were old. The nurses had to use loud voices and speak into their ears to tell them how and when to take their medicine. It was as if the words were floating next to them, and they were pointing at them as they read.

I walked up to the reception counter to show them my insurance card and joined the old people on the benches half-watching the news. Next to me was an old woman with her hands folded over the handle of her cane. I couldn't tell if her eyes were open or closed.

They called my name and gave me a plastic badge and had me cross the lobby to the orthopedics waiting area. The nurse who greeted me had the bearing of an assembly-line worker. She spoke with her focus on my fingertips.

The ward I was sent to had more patients than anywhere else,

and almost none of them were injured in any obvious way. I followed the instructions on my intake sheet, signed my name and brought it back. Then I just stood there and waited for my turn.

When I was called into the examination room and the doctor saw my face, his eyes went wide.

"That must have hurt!"

The doctor was about my father's age, maybe a little older, with a long face and a good build. Between the discolored walls and worn-out medical equipment, his lab coat was so dazzlingly white it almost looked mint green, and the pocket at his chest was full of ballpoint pens and pencils capped with erasers.

"Did you bleed?" he asked, rolling up a chair.

"Yeah," I said.

"How much?"

"A lot."

"Yeah, I bet." The doctor nodded, skimming the intake sheet. He made sure I hadn't had a headache or felt nauseous afterwards, and asked me what part of the bike had hit my head. I said I didn't think it was the bike, but that I banged it on the ground. He hummed meditatively and rolled a little closer. He pressed my forehead with his fingers and had me drop my chin while he shined a little silver penlight up my nose and hooked my nostrils with his fingertip so he could have a look inside. I caught a hint of his breath, which almost had a sour edge to it. When he was done, he squeezed his way down my nose with careful pressure, asking me to tell him when it hurt. I said everything hurt, and felt my eyes swelling with tears, until finally one dribbled from the corner of my eye. The doctor swiveled over to his desk, causing the chair to squeak, and made an annotation on my record. He said I would need an x-ray and asked me to wait for a nurse in the hall.

A little while after the x-ray, I was called back into the examination room. The doctor pointed at the images and said my bones showed no sign of abnormality.

"Even if nothing's broken, you took quite a hit. It's probably going to sting for a while." He brought a fist up to his mouth and coughed. "But, like they say, time heals all wounds."

"I don't have to keep coming back, though, right?" I asked him cautiously.

"Come back anytime," he said with a laugh. "Nothing we can do but wait and see. We'll get you some painkillers and a compress. You can take the pills whenever it hurts, and just use the compress when you go to sleep. You can use it during the day, too, if it doesn't bother you, but just at night should get the job done."

He tapped his desk with the tip of the pen.

"The compress is big, so you'll have to cut it down to size, okay? And don't take the pain pills more than twice a day."

I told the doctor thanks and stood to go.

"One more thing," he said. "Even if the swelling goes down, I want you to sit out of gym class. Nothing physical. Your body has to heal. I'm sure your teacher will understand as soon as he sees your face." He smiled broadly, but didn't laugh this time. I could see almost all his teeth. They were perfectly straight, and big, nearly the size of his thumbnails.

"You know what, you'd better come back, in about a week. Just so I can see how things are going."

The doctor slapped his knees and told me to rest up. As if that were some kind of signal, the nurse pulled back the curtain with a smile and led me out into the hall, where she called the name of the next patient. Her voice was weirdly nasal.

CHAPTER SIX

A utumn spiraled downward, every day a little more.
One morning, after my usual walk down the tree-lined
street, I entered the schoolyard to find a kind of flower
whose name I didn't know, blooming in the beds inside the
gate. Round blossoms with giant petals of light pink and white,
popping up like carefree afterthoughts from a surface of dry
algae.

It must have been some kind of flower that only grows in
fall. But captivated as I was, I realized this was just another
marvel from a world that would never accept me. The only
feeling that was truly mine was the pain lingering in my nose.
The pain was receding, easier to handle by the day, but it felt
like my spirits were never going to lift, no matter how long I
waited for change.

Maybe halfway into October, Kojima left me a note saying
she wanted to meet. It was short. It just said to meet her the
next day after school, at our usual spot.

I found the note taped inside my desk, like the others. I
went to the bathroom to read it. Something about her handwriting had changed since the first time I saw it. The writing
was hers, but the fragile, thready letters written in mechanical
pencil had grown larger and thicker. They dug deep into the
paper. But that was her. Looking at it messed with my head.

I didn't feel great about it, but I wrote, "I'm busy tomorrow."

The next day, she wrote back saying she could meet me any
day, any time. The day after that, I found yet another note

inside my desk, this one saying she had something to tell me in person. I didn't respond to either.

I couldn't bring myself to see her.

I wasn't sleeping well.

Every morning when I woke up, the same parts of my throat and chest hurt in the same way, and when I drank some water, they hurt worse. My mind empty and my body drained, I managed to drag myself to school, but I always got sleepy and nodded off in class. My teachers yelled at me. Ninomiya and his buddies loved it. Not sleeping made my body hot the entire day. I was always sweating for no reason, and my skin was clammy.

Even at home with my mom, saying hi and bye was painful. Up in my room, I didn't touch a book, much less read one. I spent full days in bed with the curtains drawn, just lying still. My appetite gradually disappeared, as if it were being whittled away, and half of my head always felt stuffed with garbage. When I bathed, I no longer saw a point in showering first and sat down dirty in the tub of water.

"When are you going back to the doctor?" my mom asked me one morning before school. "He's a professional. If you don't do what he says, your nose will rot."

I said that I was fine and headed for the door. I realized it had actually been a long time since my only visit to the hospital.

"Know what happens to a rotten nose?" she asked me by the door.

"It falls off," I said.

"Oh, if only. It won't fall off," she cautioned. "It'll tear away. You know the difference? When it tears away—"

She was eager to continue, but I told her I knew what happened and walked out the front door.

By the end of October, not sleeping at all had become normal for me. If I slept for even an hour, I would wake up, and after that I'd be unable to fall asleep again. The rest of the night, I would sit up and look out the window, when it was still too dark to see outside, and would eventually lie down and close my eyes for a while, only to sit back up again.

The calendar on my desk said October 1991. It had been only a month. In the weak light before dawn, I lay on my back and tried to run through the last month in my mind, but I couldn't think of anything concrete.

I found myself thinking more about suicide.

At first, suicide was just a word, a vague idea separate from reality. It pointed at a way that other people chose to die, people I didn't even know. But once the word became my own, it took on the strangest shape. I could feel it growing deep inside of me. Suicide wasn't only something that happened to strangers. I could make it happen, if I wanted to.

My thoughts crystallized into plans.

I ran my fingers over my wrist where I would slice it with a knife, but the sensations—the right hand cutting, the left wrist being cut—were distant, not mine. If I actually broke the skin, I would bleed so much more than I did in the gymnasium. I didn't die that day, but when you cut your wrists, you do it to die.

I thought about taking medicine to kill myself. I would fill my throat with white pills. They'd pile up at the bottom of my stomach. I imagined the pills mixing with the acid in my stomach, and wondered how the medicine would affect my body, how it would kill me. With medicine, I thought, you probably fall asleep and never notice that it's happening. That sounded like the right way to go, but it was still so far away. I didn't know what medicine to get or where to find it, or how much I would need to take. And all I could think about was how the heat would leave my body after the pills had killed me. I'd be cold.

What is dying anyway? I let this impossible question fill the darkness of my bedroom. I thought about how somebody was always dying somewhere, at any given moment. This isn't a fable or a joke or an abstract idea. People are always dying. It's a perfect truth. No matter how we live our lives, we all die sooner or later. In which case, living is really just waiting to die. And if that's true, why bother living at all? Why was I even alive? I made myself crazy, tossing and turning, hyperventilating. Then it hit me: dying is just like sleeping. You only know you're sleeping when you wake up the next day, but if morning never comes, you sleep forever. That must be what death is like. When someone dies, they don't even know they're dead. Because they never see it happen, nobody ever really dies. This hit me like a sucker punch.

At first, my desire to die was a desire to disappear. I wanted to erase myself and feel real peace. But if dying doesn't actually involve a moment where you die, could I really disappear? Wouldn't death basically mean wandering around forever, in something like a dream? It made me wonder: who could tell the difference between living in this world and living in a dream?

I could see myself in my school uniform laid out in a coffin, my nostrils plugged with cotton. People crowding around me, in the same place as the funeral I went to. I'd have this little smile on my face. I know that if I really died, I would have no way of seeing what the world would be like after I was gone, but I couldn't resist imagining it. What would the kids in my class think? I guess it would depend on what I wrote in my suicide note, but Ninomiya and the others would probably get in trouble. Or maybe the rest of the class would cover for him. I bet some people would think I was to blame, killing myself over a little harmless bullying. No, I'm sure of it. They might even say that I was heading that way all along, and that this was what I wanted. Or that I couldn't handle it. But killing myself and leaving the world behind wouldn't fix everything. Would it save Kojima from being bullied, or just make things worse? When I closed my eyes, these thoughts rose to the surface, floating past me only to burst and disappear. No matter what happens, people will always forget. If I let myself kill myself, it wouldn't change anything.

I started crying all night long. Not really consciously crying, so much as feeling tears drip from my eyes, like when you realize that you're sweating. I couldn't stop the tears. I asked myself if I was sad, but I'd lost touch with what sadness was supposed to be. If crying means you're sad, then I was definitely sad, but isn't that the opposite of how it's supposed to go? The tears kept coming, streaming down my face. My chest pounded. Too many times to count, I sat paralyzed in bed and watched the night come to an end.

Kojima kept writing me short notes, even the occasional long one.

They were gentle. They made me wish that I could see her and talk about all kinds of things. But somehow I couldn't do it. I couldn't even write her back. Our trip last summer, and our time in the stairwell, and all the other things that insulated me were now in tatters, no longer there to keep me warm.

The words that filled the class broke apart before entering my ears. I sat all day. I couldn't remember how to be strong. Like a stranger, I observed my body weakening by degrees. Yet as my body drained, the letters from Kojima offered a strange magic, a nourishing power that kept me breathing. Whenever I read them, at least for the moment, there was nothing else.

A change was evident in how Kojima let herself be bullied. She had been as lifeless as a worn-out mattress, but now she was protected by a forcefield, like the power in her letters. Honestly, it felt as if she had made this shield herself. Not a single thing had changed about the class, but I understood that she had changed in ways nobody, not even me, could really comprehend. Sure, the girls still kicked her down and sent her off on errands, but the more of that I saw, the less I understood what I was seeing.

On the occasions when our eyes met, Kojima turned all the way around and grinned at me, from the corner of her mouth. I felt stupid for not being able to respond to her letters, but her smile told me not to worry. It was okay. She looked at me until I had to look away.

The following Thursday, I visited the hospital.

I arrived a little after five and, like the last time, found the reception area and the lobby swamped.

From the people and the colors and the programs on TV to the voices I was hearing, and especially the smells, the place looked completely, flawlessly identical. And why not? It was, after all, the same hospital, but the sameness didn't hit me in an achy way, like with nostalgia, or give me an uncanny feeling of having done this all before, like déjà vu. I knew where I was, but I didn't know when. Something weird was going on.

When I stepped forward, heading for the sign-in sheet, I saw Momose among the faces of the people seated in the lobby.

He sat in his uniform among the patients and the people waiting for their medicine, sitting alone on the bench all the way at the back.

My heart squeezed in my chest. On impulse, I ducked behind a payphone. A middle-aged woman holding the receiver between her chin and shoulder startled when she saw me, but one look at my face made her turn away. I was sure Momose couldn't see me here, but I could tell it was him. Momose. Just thinking about him made my pulse race.

It occurred to me that I had never bumped into Ninomiya or Momose or any of those guys outside of school.

What happened at school stayed at school. Wherever I went, I carried the weight of what Ninomiya and Momose and my classmates did to me, but strictly speaking, they occupied only half of my whole life. Seeing Momose outside of the confines of our school made me feel like I had wandered off the map. I knew that I should forget about seeing the doctor and slip out through the automatic doors, but I couldn't even leave the space between the lime-green payphones and the potted plants.

But a second later, I walked over to Momose. With each footstep, the rubber of my sneakers made full contact with the lobby floor, which was made from a mysterious substance that felt neither hard nor soft. Cautiously, I crossed the lobby. My head was a gravid void. I had nothing to say to Momose and had no desire to see his face. I didn't know what I was doing.

Momose was sitting at the far end of the bench, slouching with his arms folded, staring at his toes.

I was standing so close to him that my shoes and his shoes could have touched.

Securely in his field of vision, I felt his eyeline rising from my toes up to my knees, then from my knees to my thighs; at my collarbone, he took a breath and finally arrived at my face. His eyes shifted, the way the shadows of clouds pass the sun on windless days. He barely moved, except for a final tilt of his chin.

I stood there without saying anything and looked down at him.

Momose looked at me for a second or two before looking back at his feet. Eyes passive, like he was staring at one of the vaccination posters on the walls. His face reminded me of a pair of brand-new white gloves.

Taking care not to kick his legs, I stepped over his knees and took the empty seat beside him. The plastic backrest was discolored. A newspaper left on the seat, bloated and wrinkled from being read who knows how many times.

Momose didn't move or even look at me when I stepped over him. I got no sense that he was acting. This was pure, unadulterated indifference. I sat down next to him and crossed my arms, too, staring at my toes. Momose looked like he was thinking about something unrelated to me.

I sat there for a while, but reception never called his name, and had no reason to call mine.

I couldn't tell if Momose was done and waiting for his paperwork or medicine, or if he was still waiting to see the doctor. It didn't look like he was hurt, and he didn't seem sick.

For a while, we just sat there.

People fidgeted around us, as if compensating for our stillness. I sat rigidly beside Momose as the automatic doors hummed open and shut. The nurses strode across the floor in their soft-soled shoes and greeted patients with excessive formality.

I couldn't tell if we had been sitting there for only a few minutes or for much longer than that, but as time slipped away, sleepiness kept rolling over me, flattening my nerves, and fending it off was making my head hurt. I had barely slept the night before. It hit me the worst during class and again around this time in the evening. The white rubber around my sneakers blurred to gray, and I had to raise my eyebrows high to keep my eyes from falling shut.

Out of nowhere, Momose got up and walked off. I stood up and went after him. He sped ahead, making his way through the crowded room, without even turning back to look at me. I followed him through the automatic doors, outside, where the world was surprisingly dark.

Night was seeping in where only minutes earlier the light of noon had remained. A stark chill cut the air, and a gust of wind set it in motion, making the branches of the trees quiver. I saw the back of Momose's uniform slip into the stream of people heading for the door, disappearing at least twice as fast as he was actually walking, as if he were being sucked into the coming night.

I chased after him, practically jogging. The hospital had a lot of land. The bike area alone was vast, and the countless bicycles parked there resembled a continuous metallic slab. Little bluish post lights were set at even intervals into the landscaping, with benches between them. Just as Momose was about to reach the gate, I caught up with him and watched myself grab him by the collar and pull hard.

Momose swung his arms against the darkening blue, catching himself with one hand on the asphalt. He looked at me for a second, then he turned away, and stood up silently to brush himself off. He stared at me, without exactly facing me. I didn't look away this time and stared right back.

"What?" Momose said, hands stuffed into the pockets of his blazer. His neck was slightly cocked. I don't think I had ever heard his voice so close before. It sounded totally different from the voice that I remembered. When I didn't answer, he repeated himself. "What?"

"We need to talk," I said, despite having nothing in particular to say.

"We? Like, you and me?" His expression didn't change.

"Yeah," I said.

"No we don't."

"Yeah we do," I said.

"No, we don't."

He was looking at my face now. I stared back at him, feeling stupid about what I had said. My knees and fingertips were twitching.

"What makes you think I have to listen to you?" he asked.

"You don't," I said.

"Whatever you think you have to say can wait. It's not like we had an appointment." He was smirking.

"I knew you'd be here," I said. "I saw you walk in." Which was a lie. "I need to talk to you."

Momose paused for effect and examined my face. I heard him let out a quick breath.

"Weirdo," he laughed. "How long is this going to take? More importantly, does this have anything to do with me?"

"We just need to talk."

"Fine, go for it." Momose walked over to the bench below the nearest lamppost and took a seat. I didn't sit down this time.

"I can't sleep," I finally told him. I had nothing to say, much less an agenda, but those words spilled off my tongue as if he wasn't there. In my head, I repeated the words. I can't sleep. What I said was true. I wasn't sleeping. "I haven't slept for like a month."

"Wow." Momose looked at his hands in his lap, at his fingertips. "So you're having trouble sleeping?"

"Yeah," I said. "I am."

"Wait, what's that got to do with me?" His face suggested that he really didn't know.

"It's because of you guys."

"What do you mean by you guys?" Now he looked genuinely perplexed.

"You know, you guys," I said.

Momose nodded and scratched at the corner of his eye.

"Okay, let's pretend I know who you're talking about. What did we supposedly do?"

Bully me, I almost said, but couldn't spit it out. There was something wrong with putting it this way. I swallowed my spit and gritted my teeth and took a deep breath. I wanted to say look, you guys are ruining my life, but it felt like this expression would fail to capture the position I was in, and what Momose and the other guys were doing to me. Unable to come up with anything appropriate, I said nothing.

"Come on," Momose said. His voice was vanilla. "Spit it out."

"You guys," I said, hiding my trembling fingers in the pocket of my blazer, "are hurting me. Like, all the time."

"Hurting you?"

"Like when you make me do things, and kick me or punch me. You hurt me because of my eye."

"And you want it to stop? That's what you're telling me?"

"Maybe."

"Maybe?" Momose laughed. "What the hell is maybe?"

"Why . . ." I said, but I couldn't say the rest. As I sat there, silent, Momose sighed at me and asked me what was up, losing his patience.

"Why do you do it? No one has the right to hurt anybody else. No one." I measured the shape and heft of each word. "I didn't do anything to deserve this."

Momose folded his hands and gazed at my knees.

"I don't care if you think I look weird. This is how I am. I'm not asking you to think I'm normal."

As I put the words together, saliva gathered at my gums, but my mouth somehow felt dry, and I had to keep licking my lips. Sitting up in the bench, Momose brushed his nails with his fingertips.

I swallowed a mouthful of spit and continued.

"Nobody does. They either look at me like I'm a freak or turn away. I'm used to that. And you guys can think whatever you want, but I just wish you would leave me alone . . . it's not like I chose to be born this way. You didn't choose to be born with normal eyes, either. In that way, we're the same, you and me. I can't help it that you think I'm disgusting. And that's fine. Still, that doesn't mean you have a right to hurt me, or anybody else."

My hands shook visibly inside my pockets. To calm them, I clenched my fingers into claws. I heard a group of girls walking their bikes behind us, chatting away.

"I don't follow," Momose said, one eyebrow raised. "I don't get it."

"Which part?" I asked.

"Well, first off," he said, "when you said that we're the same, you were way off. See for yourself. I'm not cross-eyed, and I'm not you. You are cross-eyed, and you're not me."

He laughed.

"We couldn't be more different. Second, that thing you just said, about how no one has the right to hurt anybody else. How we should leave you alone because you didn't do anything? I don't understand that."

"What's so hard to understand?" I asked.

"Nobody does anything because they have the right. They do it because they want to."

Momose cleared his throat and strummed the joints of his pointer finger as he spoke.

"What was that other thing you said? You said we do it for no reason, right? I agree with that, but so what? What's wrong with that? I mean, if you want us to leave you alone, you're totally free to want that. But I'm totally free to ignore what you want. That's where things don't add up. You're mad that the world doesn't treat you like you want to be treated, right? Like, right now is a good example. You can walk up to me and say you want to talk, but that doesn't mean I have to listen. Know what I mean?"

I replayed inside my head what Momose had just said and looked at his hands.

"More than that, though," he said. "I got to tell you. This whole thing about you looking the way you look. You make it sound like that's why we act the way we do, but that's got nothing to do with it."

His words injected lead into my bloodstream.

Nothing to do with it? I could hear my heart pulsing in my throat. I felt a suction deep inside my ears. I nervously licked my lips, breathed in and out again. When I spoke, my voice was strained.

"What's that supposed to mean?"

Momose looked at me and laughed like he thought it was funny.

"It means you got it wrong. I know you get bullied at school. It's not like I live for it, or even enjoy it. Who cares? Like, I know everyone laughs at you, kicks you, punches you, and I know it happens every day. You're not wrong about that part. And your eyes are messed up, so everyone calls you Eyes. That's true. But it's just a coincidence. Your eyes have nothing to do with what happens at school. That's not why you get bullied."

"I don't know what you mean," I said. "You guys are always . . . making fun of my eyes, saying stupid things about them. Calling me Eyes and beating me up. Now you're saying that's not why?"

"Listen, listen." Momose laughed at me. "There's no reason it has to be you. It could have been anyone. But you happened to be there, and we happened to all be in a certain mood, so things went the way they did."

"I don't know what you mean." It took everything I had just to repeat myself.

"What part don't you understand?" Momose asked. "No one's picking on you because of your eyes. That's all I'm saying." He let out an exasperated breath.

"Then why is it me, out of everyone in class?"

I was unsure if I should say the next part, but I said it.

"You guys are always picking on Kojima, too. You call her dirty and beat her up for how she looks. If it's really a coincidence, why is it always the two of us? Why are we being punished?" My voice shook worse than my hands.

"Kojima?" Momose looked askance at me. "Oh, her."

A blast of wind shook the trees.

"Think about it, though," Momose said. "Coincidence is all there is. That's how the world works. I'm not just talking about you getting bullied. Does anything in the world ever happen for a reason? Pretty sure the answer's no. Yeah, once it's happened, you can come up with all kinds of explanations that look like they make perfect sense. But everything starts from nothing. Always. You were born for no reason, and the same for me. There's no reason for us to be here. But there are these, I don't know, tendencies. Sometimes you just want to do something. You get these, like, urges. Like you want to punch someone, or kick someone, whoever happens to be there. The only reason those things happened to you is that you were around when someone was looking for someone to punch. That's all."

"That's all?" I repeated the words without grasping their meaning.

"Yeah, that's all. I don't give a crap about you. I couldn't care less what Ninomiya and the others do to you. I might be there, but I'm not thinking about it. I have no opinion on the matter. It doesn't do anything for me. So, for me, yeah, that's all."

"So you don't even think," I said softly, "you don't think it's bad to treat people this way?"

"Hold on." Momose sighed at me again. "You think this is about what's good and what's bad? Because that's not what I'm talking about. I'm just trying to explain the situation."

I couldn't move or speak. No idea how to respond, I stood there staring at Momose's knees. He strummed his fingers.

"None of this has any meaning. Everyone just does what they want. They have these urges, so they try to satisfy them. Nothing's good or bad. There was something they wanted to do, and they had the chance to do it. Same goes for you. I'm sure that when you want to do something, if you can manage it, you're doing it, right? Same principle."

"You're wrong," I blurted out. I scratched my fingernails

together in my pockets. "You're just seeing things the way you want to see them. It's not the same at all. There's a big difference between, like, going somewhere you've been wanting to go and punching someone for no reason."

"I'm not saying they're the same thing. Just the same idea. Know what I mean?"

"You know better than that," I said. "You know what you're doing is wrong."

"I don't know," Momose shrugged. "But honestly, who cares?"

"Then why do you guys always do it so nobody finds out?" I asked. "It's because you feel guilty. That's why you always tell me to keep my mouth shut and hide everything from the teachers . . . That's why you never leave any marks on me. If it's a natural urge, why can't you do it in front of everybody? Because you know it's wrong. That's why you can't do it in plain sight."

"Why should we?" Momose made a face like he was missing something. "What difference would it make?"

"Because," I said. "If you believe it's right, you should be able to."

"I thought I told you, it's not about right and wrong," Momose said. "Are you listening? No one does anything because it's right. That's not why people do things."

"That isn't . . . that isn't true."

"Yeah it is."

I sighed. Looking up at him, I shook my head. The air was growing noticeably cooler, and the sky had gotten dark. If I squinted, I could see white bugs flying at the edges of the light. I took off my glasses and rubbed my eyes, attempting to remember all of the things Momose had said. It didn't go so well. All I could do was stand there. "If you were me," I said, "and someone else was saying all this stuff to you, you think you'd believe them?"

"What makes you think I want you to believe me? There's no need for you to agree with me. You're free to think whatever you want."

"That's why I—"

"Hear me out, though. There's no beautiful world where everyone thinks the same way and they all understand each other perfectly. It doesn't exist. You think it does, but it's not real. When you really look at what's going on, everyone's living in their own world. They come into contact . . ."

"That's your—"

Momose kept going.

"When our worlds come into contact, it might look like they're connected, but they're not. It's like you said before. You thought you get bullied because of your eyes. To me, though, that doesn't make any sense. I don't care if things are so bad that you can't sleep. That's got nothing to do with me. It doesn't make me feel anything. Nothing. Your problems have never crossed my mind. It's not even bullying to me. And I'm not just talking about the two of us. It's like this for everyone. Things never go the way we want them to. But your desires have no effect on what happens out there in the world. We're all caught up in our own personal values, trying to get whatever we want."

He cleared his throat and went on.

"All I mean is, if you want it to stop, your only option is to do something to us. To Ninomiya. Like I said, it doesn't matter to me. I get nothing out of it. But, in the moment, something comes to me. An idea. An opportunity presents itself. That's also why we're standing here talking, right?"

"Then what about how people feel?" I muttered, mostly to myself.

"What about it?" said Momose. "Isn't it pretty obvious that no one else is going to look after your emotions? Don't try to tell me something stupid like it's my responsibility to think about your feelings. Who does that?"

Momose laughed out loud. I was speechless, watching him laugh and laugh. He couldn't stop.

"It's all the same. Art, war, whatever. This tastes good, that thing's beautiful. This is real, that's a lie. It's all people ever talk about. There's no end to it. It just keeps going. People can't shut up, though, because that's what life is all about. It doesn't matter if it's making them angry or happy, people enjoy that crap."

Momose shrugged and cracked his neck.

"Sometimes, though, those urges scare the hell out of me," he said, "and no one's around to protect me from myself."

Momose cracked up. He thought this was hilarious, and laughed so hard his hair kept falling in his eyes. He brushed it back and laughed some more. His white teeth flashed between his lips.

"Hey, how long are we going to talk?"

I didn't know how to respond.

"I think I gave you a decent explanation," he said, with a smile on his face.

I looked him right in the eye.

"What would you do if I killed myself?"

Momose laughed out loud again.

I didn't let this stop me.

"What if I left a note, saying everything you did? Every single thing."

"Well," Momose said, done laughing for the moment. He looked at me. "I guess that'd be annoying, but why should it bother me any? We're just kids. Nothing's a crime at this age. It'd blow over in no time. Bullying isn't black and white. Things like that are all about interpretation."

"Don't you feel guilty?" I asked.

"Guilty?"

"I don't mean when you're with Ninomiya and them. When you're alone, don't you feel guilty about what you've done?"

"Nope," he said.

"But if you had someone in your family going through this, you'd be hurting."

"Hell yeah, I would." Momose's face surprised me. "What kind of monster do you think I am? Not sure if you know this, but I have a little sister, and I love her more than anything. I'd never let something like this happen to her."

"See? How can you do something to me that you'd never want done to your own flesh and blood?"

"Those two things have nothing to do with each other. Why can't I do things to people that I don't want other people doing to my sister?"

Momose opened his eyes wide and looked right at me.

"If you don't like it, stopping it is up to you and no one else. It's that simple. You should know that this rule about treating others the way you want to be treated is bullshit. Total bullshit. It's just this thing that people with no power and no talent tell themselves. Wake the hell up."

He laughed.

"Come on," he said, "think about it. Like, check this guy out." Momose pointed behind me with his jaw. I turned around and saw a family of three walking toward the gate. The parents were probably in their mid-forties and their daughter had to be a little older than us. She was wearing a high school uniform.

"I don't know the first thing about him, obviously. But if his daughter were, you know, getting naked in videos or banging random dudes for extra money, you and I both know what his reaction would be. We can all keep our emotions down most of the time, but there are some things that bring it all to the surface. We both know this dude watches girls getting fucked on porno tapes and goes places where he can fuck girls in real life. He does it like it's normal. But guess what? All those girls have fathers. When he spreads a girl's legs, do you think it crosses his mind that she's someone else's little girl? Hell no.

But that's what it would mean to put yourself in someone else's position, right? I know, I know. Not the same thing, right? Not even close. But I promise you, no guy's thinking about how the girl's dad feels when she takes off her clothes or opens her legs. Don't get me wrong, though. That's not a bad thing. Good and bad don't enter into it. Everyone does whatever they feel like doing, whatever works."

He rubbed his eyes as he went on.

"For people to actually live by some golden rule, we'd have to be living in a world with no contradictions. But we don't live in a world like that. No one does. People do what works for them, whatever makes them feel good. But because nobody likes getting stepped on, people start spouting crap about being good to others, being considerate, whatever. Tell me I'm wrong. Everyone does things they don't want people doing back. Predators eat prey, and school serves no real purpose other than separating the kids who have what it takes from the ones who don't. That's the whole point. Everywhere you look, the strong walk all over the weak. Even those fools who think they've found the answers by coming up with perfect little sayings about how the world ought to be can't escape it. Because the real world is everywhere."

"So it makes no difference?" My face was heavy. "We should go through life doing whatever we want?" My voice was so quiet that there was no way to tell if I was talking to Momose or talking to myself.

"When you were a kid," he said to me, "people probably told you that you would go to hell if you were bad, right?"

I didn't answer him.

"Well guess what, there's no hell. It's all made up. They made it up. Nothing had any meaning, so they had to make some. The weak can't handle reality. They can't deal with the pain or sadness, let alone the obvious fact that nothing in life actually has any meaning." He laughed.

"No one thinks that." I could barely get the words out.

"Except for anyone with a normal brain," Momose said, laughing right at me. "Listen, if there's a hell, we're in it. And if there's a heaven, we're already there. This is it. None of that matters. And you know what? I think that's fucking great."

I stared back at him.

"Stop feeding yourself these stupid lies," he said. "There's nothing you can do but protect yourself."

"What if . . ." I let out little breaths, in an attempt to purge the chaos from my head. "What if I said I was going to kill you?"

"I'd say do it, if you think you can." He didn't hesitate. "You do what you can. Do whatever you want. No one's going to get in your way. No one has the right to stop you. Here's the thing, though. You've never killed any of us, even though you've had lots of chances. Okay, killing is a little extreme. But, like, think about what happened that day when we stuffed your head inside a volleyball and kicked you around. We did that. But you could never do it back. Why not? That's the problem. Maybe you tell yourself there were too many of us, but that's not it. What if I said you could put a volleyball over my head and kick me as hard as you wanted? That I wouldn't be mad, and I wouldn't even kick you back. You think you'd do it?"

"I don't—" I started to talk, but spit blocked my throat. I swallowed and started over. "I don't want to."

"See?" Momose said with a grin on his face. "That's your problem. Is it because you don't want to, or because you can't? What's stopping you from coming at us with a kitchen knife? If you tried, things would change, but you still can't do it. Why? Are you afraid of getting caught? You could do it now and it wouldn't even be a crime."

"It doesn't matter if it's a crime." My voice made my entire body shake. "I just don't want to."

"Because you'd feel guilty? Okay, but if we don't feel guilt, what makes you feel it? Which one of us is right?" Momose laughed. "Guess what? They're exactly the same."

I was quiet.

"All that matters is that you can't do it. You can't. That's why you've never said you'd kill us or whatever, even after we made you into a soccer ball. You've never done anything, because you can't. Some people in this world can do things, others can't. At cram school, there's this rich kid, and some of the other kids make him bring money from home every day. Some people get a kick out of making people jerk off in front of them. We're not like that. I'm not saying one's better than the other. It's just that some people can do things, and others can't. There are things that they want to do and things that they don't. Everyone has their own likes and dislikes. It couldn't be any simpler. People do what they can get away with."

Momose suppressed a yawn.

"None of it happens for any reason, though. We can do those things, for no reason. We can. We do. And you can't. There's no reason for that, either. That's how it is, at least for now. Six months from now, a year? Who knows? Who cares?"

CHAPTER SEVEN

I came to my senses when the nurse called my name.

She led me back to the examination room. The doctor came in, took a look at my nose and asked if I was feeling any better.

"Listen, we can't make you come unless it's an emergency, but you need to stay on top of things." He chuckled. I told him I was sorry.

"Lucky for you, it's healing pretty well. Almost there." He brought his face close to mine and scanned my features like he was drawing a circle around my nose with his.

"Does it hurt?"

"Not really, not anymore."

"Good thing you didn't break it."

"I know," I said.

"Did you take the painkillers?"

"Just once, at night."

The doctor nodded sagely, then swiveled his chair toward his desk.

"You know, it would have been a whole lot worse if it were broken." He turned away to write something in my record. "When I was in my teens, maybe a little older than you are now, I broke my nose."

He spun around and pinched his nose between his thumb and forefinger.

"I got in a fight. My nose was bent all the way to the side. When we were throwing punches, I was too caught up to notice. Later on, though, when I saw my face in the mirror, I couldn't believe it. It's not something you see every day, your own nose pointing the wrong way like that. I almost lost my mind. Most of the time, you look in the mirror, and your nose is right where it's supposed to be, but what I saw was right out of a Picasso. You know what I mean? My mom took me to see the doctor, but he was a quack. Honestly, most doctors back then had no idea what they were doing. My nose was still bleeding, but this guy shoved a rod, sort of like a chopstick, right up my nose to set it straight. He just jammed it up there. No anesthetic, obviously. Thinking about it gives me the chills, even now. See? Goosebumps."

He rolled up the sleeve of his lab coat and motioned for me to take a look. I looked, and there they were.

"After that, it wasn't so different from your situation. The doctor told me to wait it out, but the pain lasted for a solid year. In bed at night, if my blanket even brushed against my nose, it hurt like hell. Doctors did things differently back then. As long as the bone healed, it was a victory. That's why my nose is crooked to this day."

Now that he mentioned it, I could see that his nose was a little off center. But compared to other people's noses, whatever that means, I thought it was fine. It rose proudly from the space between his eyes without apology.

"Such is life." He laughed. "Take good care of your nose."

"I know," I said. "I only get one."

"That's right!" he laughed. "One is all you get."

The doctor told me the pain should go away soon, but that I could always come back if anything came up.

When I thanked him and got up to leave, he asked me one more thing.

"How long has your eye been that way?"

I looked back, paralyzed.

"No plans to have that taken care of?"

He seemed untroubled by my lack of a response. The nurse stood by the door, holding the curtain back for me to go, her eyes on the doctor too. Unable to answer, I stood beside her, looking back at him.

"Doesn't it make things hard for you? Some people get pretty bad migraines."

I nodded quietly and closed my eyes. A faint ringing passed through my ears and left in its wake an inexorable silence. I noticed how thick and dry my tongue was in my mouth and wished I had had something to drink after my talk with Momose.

"One time," I began, "when I was little, I had surgery. But my eye went back to how it was before."

"How young were you?" the doctor asked.

"Five," I said.

"Maybe you should give it another try," the doctor said, like it was nothing. "I can't say for sure, but it sounds like you were dealing with an amateur."

He almost laughed, but stopped himself.

"Kidding, kidding. You just have to find the right person for the job. It's a simple procedure, but it's also very delicate. It's the sort of thing they have young doctors try right out of med school."

"But they had to give me a general anesthetic," I said. It didn't sound like my voice saying it.

"Only because you were so little," he laughed.

"Is it the sort of thing that you can do again?" I asked cautiously, swallowing whatever spit was in my mouth.

"Depends. But it shouldn't be a problem in your case. Some people need a few rounds for things to take," he explained. "If you did it now, a local anesthetic would be fine. There isn't much to the surgery, really. They just tug on your eye muscle a little bit and let it slip back into place. Doesn't take long. Still, some younger doctors don't pull hard enough and others pull too hard. That's what I mean. You have to find the right person for the job. Lucky for you, we have a pro in-house, in ophthalmology. Talk it over with your mom. And just to confirm," he added, "You've had binocular vision in the past, right?"

"I've had a lazy eye since I was three," I said tentatively. "I don't really remember what it was like before, though."

"In that case, you should be fine," he said, scratching his head hard enough I could hear it. "We had a boy a little younger than you, not long ago. He said he wanted to play pro baseball. But when your eyes are like that, you're not going to be out there catching pop flies."

"Nope," I said.

"Maybe you're not aiming to play in the majors, but if you take another spill and really break your nose, you'll be in a world of pain. As it stands, between surgery and rehab, you'll still have to spend a little time here, but I think it's worth it." He drummed his fingers in a marching rhythm on his desk. "The choice is yours, of course."

"Okay," I said, but wasn't sure what to say next. The nurse stood beside me, holding the trim of the curtain, looking to me then to the doctor.

"It doesn't cost much, by the way," he added, after a pause.

"Really?" I said, far louder than I meant to. I had never asked how much we paid for the operation that I had when I was five and knew basically nothing about what had been done, but I could feel a change in the air. It felt strangely unsettling to know I could be normal. With a simple operation, they could fix my eye—I had never imagined such a thing was possible. I had assumed that my failed experience with surgery meant my eye would be this way as long as I lived. My eye could be . . . normal? I couldn't believe it. It was unbelievable. I stood there, unable to suppress the heaving in my chest. I placed a hand over my mouth and found myself biting my nails. I couldn't think of what to think of next. Momose's face appeared before me. His silhouette against the cool light of the lamppost. I remembered the dim light of my bedroom, and the sight of my reflection. In the mirror, only my tired left eye could find its counterpart. My right eye, same as always, lapsed toward the corner, and if I put my finger right in front of it, I saw no more than a blur of skin.

"If you're interested," he laughed, "set up a time. It's a cheap fix."

"How much," I said, struggling to produce the words, "would it cost?"

He crossed his arms and closed his eyes, making a face like he was putting everything together in the space behind his forehead. He hummed a little before he spoke.

"You're looking at 15,000 yen."

"15,000 yen," I said.

"I can't believe it's the middle of fall already," Kojima said. She looked at me and laughed.

Once we were in November, the wind turned cold. Kojima's blazer smelled vaguely chemical. It made me think of winter. Smells can remind you of all kinds of things. More than remind, they bypass your mind altogether, tingling your palms and nose, triggering feelings before they even become feelings.

I had been nervous since the night before about the two of us meeting up after so long; while I waited for her in the fire stairwell, I couldn't calm my nerves. It made me remember the very first time we met up at Whale Park. The kind of evening you can watch descend, the blue sky darkening into night before your eyes. It felt like it had happened in another life, but it had happened that same year, just in a different season.

"I know we haven't talked that much, but I've actually been okay."

Kojima leaned into the railing, turning her back on the sunset sinking into the horizon, where the town below us met the sky. As she spoke, she kept crossing and uncrossing her arms.

I had gotten this impression from seeing her around at school, but seeing her up close for the first time in so long, Kojima looked skinnier. Not like she was heavy before. The baby fat was gone from around her chin and what I could see of her arms and legs. It felt like she was someone else. Her uniform looked baggier than usual. Judging from her expression and complexion, she seemed tired. Physically, at least. But underneath her eyebrows, her eyes were fiery and cool at the same time, sharper than I remembered them. Sometimes she twisted and tugged at her hair. It was getting really long, like she was growing it out. Her split ends splayed like the straw of a broom. Her hair had flecks of lint in it. Things look so different close up.

"I read your letters," she said, "like, over and over. They always made me feel better. What about you? Did you read mine?"

I said I did. Kojima nodded, smiling with satisfaction. I couldn't bring up not being able to respond, and Kojima didn't ask.

"Know what? Even though we didn't meet or talk or whatever, I feel like I always knew how you were feeling." This made her laugh. I didn't know how I should respond to this, so I waited a second and asked if she had lost weight.

"Uh-huh," she said, and added that she hadn't been eating much lately.

"You can't eat?" I asked.

"It's not that. It's a sign, a new one," she said.

"A new sign?"

"Uh-huh," she said, grinning a little.

"But you have to eat," I said.

"I do," she said. "Just not that much." Kojima trained her eyes on me. "Not eating means something to me now."

"As a sign?" I asked again.

"Right, as a sign."

"Like a sign with your dad?"

"Exactly," she said. "Except the meaning of the signs has kind of changed for me."

"Changed how?" I asked.

"Well, at first, I think it was a way to not forget my dad. Like, my dirty gym shoes were like my dad's shoes. The same with my skin. As long as I didn't bathe, my skin was like his skin, and I could keep his smell close. But that's not it, not anymore. I mean, I've learned that what I have with my dad, it isn't just about memories. It's not just about remembering. What I mean is . . . it's a beautiful weakness. That's what we're protecting, always, each in our own way. It's what we fight for."

She spoke as if pressing each word into my palm. She looked like a picture against a backdrop of expanding darkness.

"It's the only thing that we can do. And not just for our sake, you know? It's for the other kids, too, even if they don't realize it. But that doesn't matter. All that matters is we understand it, you and me. We get it. And, like, in that way, living with this weakness, accepting it completely, that's the greatest strength in the whole world. It's not just my dad or them or us. We do it for everyone who's weak everywhere, in the name of actual strength. Everything we take, all of the abuse, we do it to rise above. We do it for the people who know how important it is. That's why I'm not eating. That's what not eating means."

Kojima stood directly in my line of sight, staring at me as she spoke.

"And I think you share that with me, you understand it,

more than anyone else. You look like you lost some weight, too. I guess you haven't been eating much, either. You really do understand. You understand what I'm thinking."

"For me," I started to speak, but stopped myself. Kojima noticed and smiled, like she was saying there was nothing to be sad about. Wind blew straight through the stairwell, and a moment later, I could smell her. Never, not even when we were side by side, had her smell been so apparent. It was the smell of not washing for days on end. I looked down, staring at the tips of my shoes.

"They all matter to me," she said. "My dad and everyone else who has the strength of weakness with them in their suffering. But you matter the most. More than anyone, it's you." She smiled. "Hey, your nose looks good."

"Yeah," I said.

"It looks like it used to," she said. "It was real messed up . . . that day."

"I know."

"What if you broke it? Would the bone pop out?"

"It turns to the side."

"No way."

"Seriously."

"I don't know," she laughed. "Maybe with a good nose like yours. A little one like mine would probably just get smushed."

"I think it would still break, though," I said.

I didn't know where to begin about the hospital, but Kojima was listening, so I dove right in, saying how I hadn't been there in years, and how the doctor who saw me was this really nice guy who actually broke his own nose when he was our age, except his insane doctor shoved a chopstick up his nose and snapped the bone back into place. I left out running into Momose and everything we said. I wanted to tell her, but I didn't have the guts, and I wasn't sure it would be wise to try.

At home and at school, I wrestled constantly with what Momose said. At times I managed to convince myself that all of it was crap, but other times I saw that he was right. I swung between these incompatible conclusions, unable to tell which one was true. I was haunted by a certainty that there was some essential, fatal flaw in the basis of my thinking, a guarantee that any thought, by virtue of its premise, would be mistaken.

Still, Momose's argument had more weight than I cared to admit, and the fragments of righteousness that had held me up weren't fitting together. Momose watched me from a dark and quiet rocky place, just smiling, staring at me, like he did that night on the bench.

I thought about Kojima.

Kojima had told me over and over that everything happens for a reason. Every time we met, her presence assured me that together, we were strong enough to overcome this. She wrote me letters. No one else had ever reached out to me like this before. And whether or not we were meeting, she was always trying to help me make it to a brighter place. Even when I couldn't make myself respond, she gave me the benefit of the doubt and sent me letter after letter. And she told me that she liked my eyes. Nobody in my entire life had ever told me that. Just Kojima.

But after what happened that day in the gym, I hadn't been able to look directly at her. The more Kojima cheered me on, and the more she cultivated that strange power, inexplicable considering how they bullied her, the harder it was to look her in the eye. I wasn't sure why. I thought back to how comforted I was, back when the days were hot, by how she talked and how she smiled. I felt a burning in my lungs. Kojima was changing, and watching it happen from a distance petrified me. The changes she was going through had rolled in unannounced, surrounding the small but persistently bright space she had created for me, pushing me out.

Wanting to communicate for the first time in forever, I had written her a letter.

"Hey, you there?" she said, scanning my face for signs of life.
"I'm here."
Kojima was giving me her take on my visit to the hospital. Although there was no one else around, she had switched over to a quiet voice, and when the wind kicked up I couldn't hear her anymore. Kojima would come closer, face to face with me. She had so many different smells. I smelled her saliva, and her sweat, and something tart. She asked me if I knew why a hospital that big had no maternity ward. I said I didn't, and she said of course not, you're not even trying, laughing but pretending to be mad. She told me about an accident at that hospital about ten years back. I nodded as she spoke, just looking at her.

Skinniness made her seem like a different person, but she looked like she was having a good time. She was alive, and seeing her like that infused me with a loneliness and indescribable longing.

"Hey Kojima," I said when her story came to an end. "I wrote to you because I wanted to talk."

"Yeah, I know," she said. "Just seeing you, though, I feel, I dunno, happamine."

Hearing that word made me want to cry. Kojima looked at me, a bit perplexed, but then she laughed. The lines of her face were new to me. I clenched my teeth and tried to keep calm. "There's something I wanted to tell you."

"You can tell me anything," she said.

"It's about my eye."

It was like the laughter animating her eyes and lips had instantly evaporated. She looked at me like she was witnessing a rare event. This made her nod, but the response was automatic, a reflex.

I told her what I had found out. That if I went through surgery there was a chance that my eye could be fixed.

Kojima listened quietly, but even after I was done she didn't speak. The air was cooling noticeably, and it was drizzling. You couldn't see the rain, but it came through on the breeze and wet our cheeks. I shrugged my shoulders, then stuffed my hands into my pockets. Kojima, standing, did the same, shoving her hands into her blazer.

"You're going to get wet," I said. "Come over here."

Kojima didn't acknowledge this.

"So . . ." she said, before going silent.

I was silent, too, waiting for her to speak.

"So you're gonna do it?" she asked, after a long pause, almost talking to herself.

"I'm not sure yet."

"Then what are you telling me for?" she asked. "You want my advice?"

"No, that's not it," I said. "I just wanted to tell you, like, what I found out."

"What for?" she asked. "What difference does it make?"

"Well," I said, but couldn't find the words. I licked my lips repeatedly, trying my best to settle down, and finally continued. "You told me you really liked my eyes."

Neither of us said anything.

"So you're gonna do it," Kojima repeated, eyes on the floor of the stairwell. "You . . . you really don't understand anything."

"Maybe. Maybe I don't . . ."

"Not maybe. You don't."

She looked at me.

"Your eyes are your most important part. They make you who you are. No one else has your eyes. I wasn't born with a sign, so I had to make my own. But your eyes were a gift. Now you want to throw that away, the thing that brings us together?"

"It still does," I said. "I don't even know if I'm going to do it. I just wanted to tell you that I found out that I might be able to fix my eye."

"Liar," she said. "I bet you were psyched when you found out. You're gonna do it and run away."

"Run away?" I asked. "From what?"

"From everything," she said. "School, yourself. This."

Kojima rubbed at her eyes with her palms.

"Don't cry, Kojima."

"You're running away from me," she said.

I shook my head.

"No, that's not what I'm saying," I said. "That's not it. I feel like I keep saying the same thing, but . . ."

"It's fine," she said, eyes on me. Her eyes were gleaming white, full of tears, quivering as she breathed. "But I'm not going to stop. I won't."

"Kojima . . ."

"I can't." The tears spilled from her eyes. "If that's what you want to do, go fix your eyes and follow the other kids. Then they'll leave you alone. And if that's what you want, there's nothing I can say, nothing I can do."

"You think that if I fix my eye, that means I'm following Ninomiya and the others?" I asked.

"Of course it does," she said. "This isn't just about us."

I looked back at her in silence.

"Even if something happens to us, even if we die and never have to deal with them again, the same thing will happen to someone, somewhere. The same thing. The weak always go through this, and there's nothing we can do about it. Because the strong never go away. That's why you want to pretend to be like them, isn't it? You want to join them. You really don't get it. You're being tested. Overcoming this is all that matters. It's what we've always talked about. It's what we talked about."

"Kojima, please . . ."

She pursed her lips. The sound of her sniffling filled the stairwell. The apparently limitless stream of tears disturbed me. Neither of us spoke for a long time. I could hear an ambulance siren in the distance. A little kid was crying barely within earshot. Kojima stood there, saying nothing, minute after minute.

"I thought," she finally said, "I thought we were friends."

"We are friends," I said. "We are."

"No, we're not. We can't be."

"Of course we can."

She shook her head decisively.

"Kojima."

"You're obviously gonna go through with it." She was crying. The tears had changed her voice.

"Kojima," I said.

"Stop. Don't say my name like that."

Her speech was breaking up. She shut her eyes and cried in silence, not letting me hear her. The effort made her shoulders jerk. Crying had never looked so painful. She clenched her jaw and clamped her thighs together. The crying made her entire body tense. Sometimes a sob burst to the surface. Snot and tears dripped from her face to the floor. I couldn't speak or move. There was nothing I could do but watch her cry.

There was nothing I could do.

When her shoulders finally came to rest, I thought that she was done crying, but that was when the sobbing started for real. I was getting desperate. I wanted to jump up and sit beside her, but I stopped myself. Her defensive posture made it clear to me that she didn't want that. So I stared at her blankly. Eventually, she spoke, but in a voice so soft I thought it was going to vanish.

"Over the summer . . ."

"Over the summer?" I said, as if to keep the words from disappearing.

"Over the summer, I told you about my mom. Remember?"

"I remember," I said.

"About how I asked my mom why . . . she married my dad."

"Yeah."

"And she said it was because she felt sorry for him."

"Yeah."

"Because she pitied everything about him."

"Yeah." I nodded a few times.

"Know what, though . . ."

Kojima lifted her head to look at me.

"You know why I'll never forgive my mom?"

The tears had dried on her grubby cheeks, and the whites of her eyes were so bloodshot they were pink. Her lower eyelids fluttered, the only pale parts of her face. She stared at me. Clumps of hair clung to her cheeks, but she didn't bother brushing them aside.

"It's not because she left my dad all alone, or even that she moved on to someone else like nothing had ever happened . . ."

I nodded.

"It's because she couldn't keep it up."

I nodded again.

"She couldn't keep feeling sorry for him. She just, she just stopped."

Kojima left me with that and walked down the stairs.

She vanished without the slightest hesitation. I couldn't speak, let alone stop her. I could hear her steps echoing down the stairwell, but not for long. As if to fill the silence she had left behind, I was surrounded by the hiss of rain. When I wasn't looking, the mist had hardened into pellets. This was the sound of a rain prepared to take no prisoners. It trembled like the cry of an unknown creature, seeming to fall from the darkening sky and rise from somewhere deep in the town.

CHAPTER EIGHT

That weekend, my mom cut herself.

She said that her hand slipped when she was washing the dishes, and a knife came down on her arm. I had been reading in my room and ran down to the kitchen when I heard the noise. She was standing with her right hand locked onto her left elbow and her left arm stretched toward the ceiling. When she saw me, she started laughing.

"Hey," she said. "It's not stopping. I'll call an ambulance."

She held her arm up high. Blood streaked into her armpit. The front of her blouse was red with blood spilling from her rolled-up sleeve onto her chest. I ran to the phone.

"Look at all the blood!" Mom said, like she thought it was a joke. I got a little angry and asked her what I should do. She had me help her tie a towel around her arm. When I started pacing, she told me to cut it out and laughed at me. While we stood there waiting for the ambulance, I realized my knees were shaking.

"They'll be here any minute. God, I don't even know how this happened," she said. "It's pretty deep, though. This is what ambulances are for. When you can't go to the doctor."

"Why are you laughing?" I asked.

"I always laugh when I get scared."

"You're scared?"

"Look at me. This is a lot of blood. Of course I'm scared. I mean, it doesn't hurt, but what do you think will happen if the bleeding doesn't stop?"

I gave it a second, then said, "You'll, uh, die?"

"Exactly," she said and nodded at me.

I heard the ambulance drive up. The doorbell rang, then two paramedics came into the kitchen and dressed the wound before taking Mom away. I wanted to go with her, but she said to sit tight, that she was only going to need a couple of stitches. They shut the front door as they left, but after a few seconds, I opened the door again and yelled after her.

"Shouldn't I call Dad?"

She turned and said, "Don't bother," waving goodbye.

I spaced out on the couch for a minute, then I got up, grabbed a rag and bucket from the bathroom and wiped up the blood on the kitchen floor. It didn't take long. There was more blood than I had realized, but I cleaned it up like any other mess. It seemed like her clothes had absorbed most of it. I was still amped up, not in the mood to read. I had no better option than to space out on the couch again.

Mom came home a little after four.

"I cut myself pretty bad," she said, showing off the white bandage wrapped around her arm.

"Did you get stitches?" I asked.

"Yeah, five." She tapped her finger up the bandage, show-ing where.

It was up to me to make us dinner. I had cooked for myself before, but never for someone else. Mom said it would be fine to order takeout, but I put something together from what we had on hand. Nothing fancy. I made white rice and miso soup and stir-fried a couple of things that were in the fridge. Mom sat the whole time and told me what to do. When I heated up some leftovers and brought them to the table, it started feeling more like a real meal.

"It's a little early, but let's eat." Mom turned on the TV and ate, like always, facing the screen. I watched too, not saying a thing.

"I'm just glad it wasn't my right hand."

"Yeah."

"All that excitement wore me out." She let out a big sigh. "I hate this kind of thing. I really can't stand it when things just happen out of nowhere."

"Yeah," I said.

"I try to keep myself calm, but I just can't do it. My body takes over. That's the part I can't stand."

"You want to stay in complete control?" I asked.

"I guess so," she said. "I can't really explain it, but it feels so violent, everything rushing up inside me. Nothing else gets to me like that."

I sat there in silence, eating my rice and cabbage. It was hard for me to tell if I was even hungry, but it seemed like I had plenty of room for more. At a certain point, it became obvious that we were done. On any other night, we would have taken our own dishes to the sink, but that night I stacked everything up at the table and carried them over myself. Mom always had a cup of hot tea after dinner. I didn't want any, but I boiled the water anyway and made her a small pot of the tea she liked.

"Hypothetically," she said, after the tea had cooled enough to sip, "how would you feel if your father and I got a divorce?"

"You're getting divorced?"

"Nothing's decided yet . . ."

I had nothing to say. Dad never came home anymore, and I couldn't care less. Back when he started coming home less often, I remember him explaining how busy he was, when I did actually see him, but that was ages ago. Which reminds me of how, one time, when I said "ages ago" in front of him, he gave me this terrible look. He said I hadn't lived long enough to talk that way about the past.

"I don't know for sure." She stopped for a second. "I know, it's crazy for a parent to ask their kid how they'd feel about them getting divorced . . . but I have a feeling that things are heading in that direction."

"Yeah," I said.

We sat there silently, eyes on the TV. I gazed into the madness of the screen without really understanding what was on. I wondered if I was going to have to move in with my dad if they got divorced. I couldn't imagine living with him, but that was probably the way things were going to play out. Even though I almost never saw him, to the point I could hardly say I knew him, he was my biological father, and apparently that mattered more than the quality of the relationship. Mom sat with her chin propped in her hand and watched the TV without saying anything. Someone was swinging upside down from a crane, dripping black ink from their hair like a calligraphy brush.

"I shouldn't have brought it up. I'm sorry. I'm not all there right now." She laughed. "God, what the hell am I doing? I'm such an idiot."

"No, it's fine," I said.

I wasn't planning to bring up my eye, but there I was, telling her how the doctor said I could be corrected with surgery.

When I was done, she was quiet for a minute, before asking me if this was what I wanted. I told her I wasn't sure.

Mom cradled the teacup in her hands, rotating it slowly. I went up to the sink to pour myself a cup of tea and brought it to the table.

"You don't have to decide anything right now. Maybe it's enough just knowing you can do it. It's a serious procedure. You'd better give it some thought."

I nodded and gazed at the steam wafting from my cup, waiting for the tea to cool down a little.

No word from Kojima.

There were no more letters, no more conversations, no

more eye contact. No matter how I looked at her, she never seemed to look back anymore. I thought about her all the time. I continued to show up early, before the others arrived, and simply waited for the room to fill, my hands inside my empty desk. It hurt to think about how this was where she used to leave letters for me. I thought about the one time she called my house. That was summer, I told myself. It was fall now.

At school, we were preparing for the cultural festival, but we also had field day coming up. Every day was packed with things I'd just as soon avoid, but the guys managed to find the time to hit me or just laugh at me when I wasn't running errands or laps for them. They never seemed to get tired of this routine. Nothing ever changed from one week to the next.

Momose never changed, either. I had thought that he might make me pay for what I did at the hospital, but there was no change whatsoever. No one seemed to know that he and I had even spoken. From the way he carried himself, you would think he had forgotten that it even happened. He was that cool.

I stopped myself again and again, but finally I wrote a letter to Kojima.

I said I wanted to meet up and talk. My failure to explain the situation with my eyes had resulted in a huge misunderstanding. I knew how important my eyes were to her, which is why I had wanted to tell her before anyone else. I apologized for doing such a bad job of explaining myself. I never wanted to hurt her.

Kojima didn't write back.

I tried writing her another letter. It was scary picking up where I left off in the first one, since she had never answered, and even scarier leaving it for her to find. I said I would be waiting in the stairwell the next day at five. I asked her to come if she could make it. I'd be there. I taped the letter inside her desk first thing in the morning. The whole day, I fixated on her body language. The next day, I got to the stairwell at five and waited for two hours, but she never showed up.

From what I saw of Kojima in the classroom, she was getting skinnier than ever. No one could have missed it. She looked like she had stopped eating entirely. Our classmates teased her about it. They weren't always direct, but they made their opinion of her clear. They laughed with lightness in their hearts.

I wrote another letter, saying we didn't have to talk about my eyes. We could talk about anything else, the way we used to. I just wanted to talk. She still hadn't shown me her picture of Heaven. I thought about that day all the time.

Like back in spring, I wrote about what was on my mind, whatever popped into my head, sometimes mentioning the books I was reading. I chose my words with care, trying to cheer her up. I got no response.

One day, between classes, Kojima got pushed hard and fell near my desk. Metal tumbled into wood. She took a few chairs and a desk down with her to the floor.

The girls laughed in their shrill voices while Kojima crouched there, motionless. I went stiff. There was nothing I could do to help her.

"Get up," one of the girls said.

The girl shoved a broomstick in the collar of Kojima's blazer so that it tugged her armpits, prompting her to stand. Kojima reeked. Head heavy, she started getting up, coarse hair covering her face. I sat there, looking at her. Once she was standing, I could see her face through her hair. It had been so long since I'd seen her face. I held my breath like I was praying and looked at her. Her cheeks were hollow. The skin around her mouth was dark. Her lips were white from peeling. In the few seconds she was standing, before the girls pulled her away, Kojima looked at me with eyes that I had never seen before.

Kojima. I heard myself saying her name, but she didn't respond. Her eyes were blank. She was smiling perfectly, at something beyond me.

Days later, I got a letter from Kojima.

I had stopped writing to her when I saw her smile that day in class. It felt so good to hear from her. I read over that sentence so many times.

She told me that she would be waiting at Whale Park that Saturday at three, in the place where we first met.

I could still remember the smell of the air on that spring evening, the hardness of the tires where we sat, the cracks in the concrete whale, the smell of the damp, black earth. Faced with this bolder version of her handwriting, I couldn't help but recall the frailness of the first note she had written to me. It hurt to remember it so completely. I felt lonely. When I got like this, I did what I always did and read through all her letters, spreading them across my desk. Those letters had so much to say. I read them over and over, then folded each one carefully along its creases before returning the whole stack to the slipcase.

That Saturday morning, my dad came home for once. He had the day off. When I came down to the kitchen, I saw him on the sofa, watching TV. When he realized I was there, he said hey, then turned back to the screen. He flicked through the channels. Each station had a different sound, a different volume.

The three of us had breakfast. We ate what Mom prepared for us without saying a word. Her bandage was bright white. Her arm and the bandage felt like an act, but I had seen the wound when it was fresh. I saw the blood. At the table, the TV did all the talking, a labor-saving device just like the dishwasher, freeing us from any obligation to converse. This is what I always thought when we were all together.

Dad read the newspaper. He folded it in half, to make it more manageable, and held it in front of his face. The sound of him folding and unfolding the newsprint made me feel nauseous. I honestly thought I was going to vomit. I felt a violent urge to snatch it out of his hands and rip it up. Hiding my disgust as I chewed, I fixated on the newspaper and fantasized about shredding every page. How would he react? I bet he'd punch me in the face without a thought. So what? Go ahead. I imagined reducing it to strips so thin that there was nothing left to tear. When I was finished with my fantasy, I wolfed down what was left on my plate and stood up from the table. My dad leaned out from behind his newspaper and looked at my place setting. I thanked my mom for breakfast and went up to my room.

I started on my math homework, but when I got sick of it I opened up the book that I was reading, and when I got sick of that I went back to math. Having Dad at home and having plans to finally see Kojima on the same day was too much for me to handle. I couldn't settle down.

I spent the morning drifting from one thing to another. After lunch, I heard Dad leave the house. A few minutes later, I went downstairs to use the bathroom and caught Mom heading out the door. She said she would be back around seven to make dinner, then she asked me if it was alright if we ate that late. I was still full from lunch, so I said no problem, then headed back up to my room. The second I heard the front door lock behind her, I pulled my thing out and started jerking off. I didn't even make it to my bed. I went at it standing in the doorway. This was new for me. I gripped it harder than usual. Vague soothing images, warm expressions swallowed me whole. Then I started to come. There was no box of tissues within reach, so I caught it in my other hand. When my palm was so full that the cum was dripping through my fingers I finally relaxed. I washed my hands then went back to my room and lay down on my bed to pick up where I had left off with my book, but I started to get hard again. I tried to ignore it, but it was too much. Sitting still wasn't working. It was like all the blood in my body was pumping into my erection. It actually hurt. All of my energy and fears and wants and needs were being fed into my penis. I stroked until it was as big and hard as it was going to get, and then I thought, for once, about Kojima.

I was doing the unthinkable.

Never had I ever thought about Kojima while masturbating. And not because I wanted to but couldn't. I didn't want to. Simple. She didn't belong in that world.

But I found myself caught in an undertow, the physics of which I could not hope to understand. Although I had no clue why this had to happen now, I couldn't make the image of Kojima go away. In a tidal surge, her image rose before me, smiling. I sat down beside her on the bench outside the art museum, leaned in, and sucked her lips. I licked the sweat off of her cheeks. It tasted unlike anything I'd ever known. I took off her uniform. Once she was naked, I put her in the tub. I washed her hair and rubbed the dirt from her body with a bar of soap. When her skin was gleaming clean, I pressed my palms against her breasts, opened her legs, then slipped inside. I cranked my hand and watched the scene unfold inside my head. I licked every part of her I could. Then I sucked her lips again. Except her face transformed into the girl I saw that time in class. She didn't look at me. Her eyes, framed by those perfect bangs, were looking somewhere else. I pulled harder, imagining myself going deeper. To the beat of my ejaculation, the face turned back into Kojima. The face I saw as the ecstasy abated was full and warm, a little puzzled, but kind, and looking at me. This was the Kojima that I wanted. When I finished, the softness and the kindness vanished. Her face grew cold. Eyes dead. Cheeks sunken. She stared at me and smiled.

She said "We're friends, right?" She told me she liked my eyes and kept on smiling. It was the smile from the last time that I saw her.

I sat up and leaned against the wall in a daze. It was a quiet and uneventful Saturday so far. I purged my lungs of heavy air and lay back down. I decided I was the worst person on the face of the planet—the grossest. What the hell was I doing? My chest glared white, while behind me a black hole was opening. I closed my eyes and waited for the feeling to subside. I heard the telephone ringing, but I couldn't move. I didn't even attempt to wipe up the cum. Before I knew it, I had fallen asleep.

I was running to the park. At an endless red light, I caught a break in the traffic and dashed across the road, almost colliding with a car. They slammed on the brakes. The driver stuck his head out of the window and called me a moron. The state I was in, I just then realized I was running. But I wasn't listening, not in any present sense. I was on a different plane, nowhere near the voice I heard. It wasn't calling me.

The sky was bright, no trace of clouds, but I could hear the rumble of thunder over the wind. When I got to Whale Park, Kojima was there. Seeing her, I stopped and bent down to catch my breath. Even though I was sweating and my chest was pounding, I had no strong sense of having run all the way here. I could have been convinced that I hadn't even left my room. But I was near the fence of Whale Park, and I saw Kojima sitting on the tires in her uniform. Taking huge breaths, which barely helped at all, I walked over to her, taking my time, wondering why she was wearing her uniform today. The ground between us was perfectly flat. I couldn't believe how many steps it took to reach her. It felt like I was walking in place, but then I was standing in front of Kojima. Kojima. I said her name. After a pause, she looked at me, as if something had just occurred to her. With her lips pursed, she blinked at me deliberately. You could almost hear her eyelashes. She cast her eyes at the ground. I was self-conscious about my heavy breathing, but I sat down next to her.

"You read my letter," I said.

Kojima didn't speak.

"The other day, you . . . that was a misunderstanding."

Winded as I was, I was trying to start a conversation. Kojima stared at the dirt, not inclined to look at me again. Even though I was beside her, I felt as if I was sleeping in my room. I could move my fingers fine, but something vital had fallen out of balance. I squeezed my eyes shut, blinking hard, attempting to clear out the space behind my eyes, but I met with a stubborn dullness, as if every crevice of my head had been packed with damp cotton, not exactly light or heavy. The space between me and things outside of me grew hazy. I became unsure of whether there was any space at all. It felt like I was dreaming. Or like I had become my eyes.

I sat there, next to Kojima, without saying any more, just staring at her knees. I reached out to touch the break in the pleats of her skirt, above her knees. I wanted to know if my hands could feel what I was seeing. My phantom fingers reached the hem of her skirt. Then I touched her hand, a little higher, in her lap. I was seeing my fingers touch the skin of her hand. It wasn't warm or cold, but it was hers—the real Kojima. Touching her brought no reaction. I sat there with my palm resting on her hand and gazed down at her dirty sneakers.

I noticed something and looked up. Momose was standing in front of us.

He wasn't alone. Ninomiya was next to him, and around them were a bunch of other faces that I recognized, smirking at what they had discovered. For a second, the smell of the gymnasium came back to me. A few girls I knew from class were with them too. Not knowing what to make of this, I counted the faces. Seven. Their expressions told me nothing. What were they doing here?

"Don't let us stop you," one of them said. He kicked me in the knee, getting mud on my jeans. One of the girls wailed with laughter.

I fixed my left eye on the knee they had kicked and touched my fingers to the streak of mud. Real mud. From a kick. He kicked me in the knee. I tried to make this sink in. I didn't feel anything like pain. I heard a rumble of laughter. A bunch of them were saying "Hurry up and do it!" Kojima stared at the ground.

"Disgusting," Ninomiya said. "So this is where you two get nasty?"

The girls cheered. The guys kicked me in the knees again. This time I definitely felt it.

"Right there?"

"Gross," one of the girls said. Some of them laughed. Momose stood apart from the group, arms crossed like Ninomiya.

"We know about you two," one of them said. "And you thought you were so smooth."

I didn't know what they were saying.

"Listen," said Ninomiya, squatting down to face me.

At eye level, his face registered as someone else, but it was a face that I knew well. When we were little, he used to say my name with those same lips, but he would say it kindly.

"I've never seen anybody do it in real life. I want you to show me."

"Show you what?" I asked. My voice was thin enough to wonder if I'd spoken. But Ninomiya heard me.

"Sex."

They all laughed. Really getting into it.

I felt something stall my breath, and replayed inside my

head what Ninomiya had just said. Sex. The word made my heart race and forced weight onto my shoulders. My thoughts jumped to the feeling I felt earlier, to what I was doing before I left the house. I heard spit rasping in my throat. My tongue went dry, and the breath rolling over it was hot. Why were they saying this to me? How did they know we were here? What did they want? What did me coming earlier have to do with them? I had no idea where to look or what to think. Momose was standing back a little, looking at me.

"Look at you two," Ninomiya stood up and laughed. "You did it at school, too, didn't you? Nice work."

He shook his head, as if genuinely impressed.

"Alright. Show me."

"We never," I started in a low voice. "We've never done it."

When I said that, everyone but Momose cracked up. What were they laughing at? All I did was answer them. I was telling the truth. I could feel sweat dripping down my back to my waist. My heartbeat thumped against my eardrums, and each beat sent a tremor through the world around me. My hand was on Kojima's. I realized I was squeezing it, but she didn't react.

"Why are you here?" I asked. My voice was raw.

"Same reason as you."

"You made her write the letter?"

"You could say that," Ninomiya laughed. "Look, man. We've got places to be. Let's get this show on the road."

One of the guys kicked me in the thigh so hard that the previous kicks felt like love taps.

"But we've never . . ." I rubbed my leg. "We've never done it."

"Dogs do it here," mused Ninomiya. "You think they give a damn? It's the same. Bet if you put your mind to it, you could do it, too. You never know unless you try, right?"

He laughed.

"We're running out of time. We've got shit to do. I need

you to hurry up. Just keep doing what you were doing. Don't be shy."

Ninomiya smiled at me with his entire face. His skin was vibrant, taut with excitement. How was this a human face? His blessed lips were tight at the corners. His eyes pinwheeled with light.

"You . . . you're crazy!"

Hearing this, Ninomiya looked at the others and burst into laughter.

"Just get on with it."

Following his orders, one of the guys yanked me up by the shoulder. I let go of Kojima, but shot out my hand to grab hold of her again. This got another laugh.

"Look, man. I'm not playing around."

I shook my head and planted myself down onto the tires. I squeezed Kojima's hand, hard. Then even harder. I dove through a gap between the guys in front of me, trying to escape, but they grabbed the back of my shirt and threw me to the ground. I was still holding onto Kojima's hand, so we fell together. I asked her if she was okay. Her eyes were wide open. She sat up and nodded, without actually looking at me. We were crouching on the ground, surrounded, fenced in by their gaze.

"Damn. Your girl's filthy. You can smell her from across the street. That's not just me, right?"

"She always smells like that," one of the girls said. She scraped the sole of her shoe against Kojima's back. "Oops, looks like I stepped in dogshit. My bad."

"Don't worry, she smelled like shit anyway."

"Hazmat. Double-bag it."

The girl was stepping on her now, pushing her forward. Kojima stopped herself from falling with her hands. I looked the girl in the face.

"Eyes and Hazmat, fucking in a tree."

They all laughed.

Kojima and I didn't move. There was plenty of light in the sky, but the pauses between the thunderclaps were getting shorter.

I asked myself if this was really happening.

Was this really happening? I knew that I woke in my room, and flew out of the house, and ran all the way here to see Kojima. I came running, like I always would, whenever she wanted to see me. Why had they crashed into our world? We had never done anything to anyone, and Kojima and I had never done anything. Never, not in all this time. But then this had to happen. I wanted to see her. All I did was come to see her. Why did we deserve to be kicked and stepped on? Why were we in the dirt?

Then I starded thinking.

This wasn't the reunion I thought it was. Kojima didn't want to see me. Ninomiya and his friends somehow found out about our letters and forced Kojima to write to me. I was the reason this was happening to her. It was my fault for writing her all those letters.

Try as I might to think this through, the words inside my head lacked any power. Kojima didn't move. I thought I felt a raindrop on my nose. I looked straight up. No rain clouds to speak of, but the sky had dimmed. The tamer light lent a different color to the air. It was a secret color, one I had seen somewhere and forgotten, almost for good, until this very moment. The air surrendered its cool edge, rounding off into thick currents of warmth that wrapped like gauze around our bodies. The thunder was audible—far away, but getting closer.

"I'll do anything. Just let her go," I said to Ninomiya. "I'm begging you. Kojima didn't want to meet me. I wrote to her. Leave her out of it. She's never even really talked to me. I just wanted to . . ."

Something blocked my throat.

I swallowed my spit and held my breath, waiting for my nerves to calm before I spoke.

Then I said it.

"It's all me."

"Bullshit," laughed one of the guys. "Your story doesn't match up with what we know."

"But I'm telling the truth."

"Look, though," Ninomiya said, his arms crossed. "Don't worry about that. Hurry up and get your pants off. I meant it when I said we're in a hurry."

"Just let her go," I said.

"Then who are you gonna do it with?" he laughed.

"Just let her go home. Please." Without realizing it, I had put my forehead to the ground before Ninomiya.

"Come on." His voice was deranged. He kicked my head softly with the toe of his shoe. "I'm no good at this emotional crap. Are you gonna take your pants off, or do you need someone to help?"

I raised my head and looked at Momose, through the dirt stuck to my glasses. I was on my knees. I said his name.

"Momose, you know this doesn't mean anything. I know you do. It doesn't matter if it happens or not, right? I know you understand. Momose, please."

Ninomiya slapped me upside the head. My glasses were hanging from one ear; my cheek was burning and a second later I tasted blood.

"Shut up. Nobody asked you to speak. Get his pants."

I kicked, trying to stop them, but the guys locked me in a full nelson and undid my belt. I heard the girls laughing. I told Kojima to run. "Go home," I screamed, wrenching my head back to see her. She just sat there. "Run!" I screamed. "Run!" I was screaming at the top of my lungs, but she just sat there.

They dropped my jeans and pulled them off me, inside out, over my shoes. Next, they ripped my shirt off and left me in my underwear. He told them to leave my shoes on, because it was funnier that way. The first girl who saw me lost her mind. "Gross!" When the other girls looked at me, they shrieked with delight. I tried to get my clothes back on, but one of the guys balled them up and put them on the concrete whale. There was no way I could get to them.

I just stood there in my underwear and sneakers, surrounded by their voices, high and low, talking like I wasn't even there. I had no sense of being hot or cold. I was distracted by the lapsing color of the sky.

"Okay, Eyes. Now help Kojima," said Ninomiya.

I couldn't believe what I was hearing.

"What are you saying?" My voice was shaking. "What did you say?"

"I said take Kojima's clothes off," Ninomiya answered calmly, then opened his mouth and raised his voice and said it again, right into my ear, to make sure I understood. "Take her clothes off."

I felt heat running through my insides, from my chest up to my throat.

Thunder rumbled through the light, and rain pattered from the sky. One of the girls complained that she was getting wet. In spite of the rain, the sun was brighter than before. If there were no clouds, where was this rain coming from? It was golden, lit by the color of the sun, spraying down in lines, hitting the back of the whale and the tires and my skin.

"If you can't do it, we'll have to do it for you," Ninomiya said. "Hey, it's raining. Hurry up."

I didn't say anything.

"You think that if you stall we'll just forget the whole thing?" he asked. "Trust me, I'm a real perfectionist. You need to finish what you start. I want results. I want them now. You hear me? You don't have a choice here. Do what I say. Now."

"I'm not gonna do it," I said.

"If you don't, someone else will," he laughed. "Plus, it's kinda hard to take you seriously when you're basically naked."

I was quiet.

The girls went on about the rain, bugging the boys. One of the girls said she was getting tired of this. I stood there in silence as their voices grew louder and louder. Ninomiya turned around and told them they could leave, if they wanted. The girls grumbled for another second or two, then changed the subject. Apparently they were staying.

"Have it your way," said Ninomiya. He told one of the guys to make Kojima stand. Without thinking, I reached for a rock in the dirt by the tires. It was big enough to need both hands. I lifted it. It was heavier than expected. I stared at the rock in my hands.

"What the hell do you think you're doing?" Ninomiya asked.

I didn't answer. I stared at the rock in my hands until its image doubled.

Half of the rock was black with moisture. It made me think of blood. The black bottom had a sharp edge. I gripped the dry half and stared at the sharp part.

I focused on what Momose had been saying to me on the bench as night set in outside the hospital. Why can't you do it? Why couldn't I do it? If I did something, maybe things would change. Maybe. But don't you feel bad? I was asking him. Nope. Not a bit. He had his answer ready. We all do what we can. That's it. No more, no less. It's meaningless. But how can it be meaningless? Momose smiled from the corner of his eyes. This isn't about being right or wrong. It is what it is. At the end of the day, what matters is what you make of it, if you can stand on other people's heads, stomp them down, force them to do as you please. I don't want to stand on your head, and I don't want you standing on mine, I screamed. It's not that simple! Momose laughed. This is what makes the world go round. This isn't some fantasy. It's reality. A simple, rigid, fully functional system. If you want to take that rock and bash Ninomiya over the head, then you should do it. Look. He's distracted. If you do it now, he'll be down for the count. Then you can finish the job. You'll feel great. You'll save Kojima. When the others see it, they'll run away. Same goes for me. You can basically do whatever you want. Who's gonna blame you? They'll sympathize, call you a hero. I say go for it. Why can't you do it? What's stopping you?

The rain was getting harder. The thunder wasn't stopping. Every minute or so, a jagged bolt would crack across the umber of the sky, lighting up the sheets of rain. Puddles were forming all over the ground. I imagined myself charging at Ninomiya with the rock over my head, but my body didn't budge. It wasn't enough. One last time, I imagined myself dropping the rock on him. But it wasn't working. I exhaled. Like Momose said. If I could, I would. This wasn't about good or bad, only whether I could or couldn't. And why couldn't I? Shouldn't I be fighting? Shouldn't I be running at Ninomiya with this rock? What was stopping me? I had a weapon. But having it wasn't enough. I had to use it. You're such an idiot. What about this is so hard for you to understand? I adjusted my grip on the rock and gathered my strength.

That was when Kojima got up and took my arm.

I looked at her.

She looked at me, but didn't say anything. Rain dripped down her face, making her eyebrows shine in the light. Her hand drifted from my arm. I couldn't speak. I looked at her and found myself wondering how many ways people had looked at me in my life. Fleeting looks, accusatory looks, humiliating looks. Total strangers had been staring at me for as long as I could remember, and I had no choice but to take it. But on a handful of occasions, I had been looked at in a loving way, like when Kojima told me that she liked my eyes. She looked me in the eye, and we held hands. This I knew. But the Kojima in front of me had no emotion in her eyes. Her eyes stared at nothing. When I looked at them, I knew.

Kojima stepped forward and stopped in front of Ninomiya.

He took a step back, but he didn't say anything. The guys hooted for a second but no more. Leaning against the whale, Momose looked our way, folded his arms again and drew in his chin.

Kojima took off her shoes and socks and stood barefoot in the dirt. Then she slipped her fingers under the collar of her shirt and undid her necktie, rolled it up and stuffed it in the pocket of her blazer. Her movements were painfully slow. Next she took off her blazer and tossed it on the ground, before undoing the buttons of her shirt, starting from the top. She unhooked her skirt. It fell to the ground, forming a navy-blue circle at her feet. The hem sank into the puddles at her feet, making the navy darker. She was down to her white tank top and her spandex shorts, navy like her skirt. She slipped them off and tossed them aside, leaving only her tank top and white underwear. The rain made the fabric stick to her skin. Rain dripped down her body in meandering patterns. No one spoke. Kojima rolled her tank top up, freed her arms, then freed her head, and tossed this to the ground too. Her ribs were popping out from her small body. She stepped out of her underwear. Now she was totally naked. No one said a word. All I could hear was the rain, falling on Kojima. The golden rain poured over her body and her discarded uniform. Light bounded from the puddles, reflecting the sun even as the rain grew harder.

Kojima stood up straight in front of Ninomiya.

Smiling.

Nobody spoke.

Never breaking her smile, she turned her naked body slowly, in a circle, stopping when she returned to Ninomiya.

Then she reached out her hands, opened her eyes wide, and exploded into laughter. It was a ruthless laugh, progressing in waves from low to high. Laughter rose out of her body as she walked toward the other classmates, making the most of every step. She went up to the girl on the far left, then cupped her palm around her cheek. The girl whose cheek she was rubbing screamed and ran away. The other girls ran after her. Still smiling, Kojima reached out to touch the boys. At first, they acted like they thought this was funny, but in seconds they were swatting at her hand and ran off too, just like the girls. They screeched and scattered, racing to beat each other out of the park. The only two left were Ninomiya and Momose. I stood there in my underwear and shoes, holding the rock in my hands, inside the golden rain, which was coming down even harder now. I was doing everything I could.

This was a Kojima I had never seen before.

Her smile had an ineffable strength, light years beyond the way she smiled after falling down by my desk.

I couldn't believe that any of this was happening. The rain was beating against Kojima's naked body and she was just laughing. She opened her hands, delirious, and reached out to touch Ninomiya. I thought I heard her say *this really matters*. Kojima. The voice I loved. I remembered how I told her in a letter how her voice was so amazing, like a 6B pencil. Then she turned to me and laughed. Hey Kojima, I said, what makes you think this matters? Of course it matters, she said. We're not giving in. We're letting it happen. And we know what's right. Our will is intact. These guys have so much more to learn. We talked about this. They'll learn someday. Kojima's laughter rang in my ears. Her smile made me miss the way things used to be. Weakness matters, she said. It has real meaning. I was silent, focused on her voice. But know what, she said, if weakness matters, then so does strength. And I don't mean weak people using the idea of strength to justify their weakness. I looked at Kojima, but when I did, I saw Momose grinning, speaking to me. If anything has meaning, everything does. And if nothing has meaning, nothing does. That's what I was saying. It's all the same. You, me, we're all free to interpret the world however we want. We see the world differently. It's that simple. That's why you need to be strong. You have to overpower people so they can't come at you with their thoughts or rules or values. No, I shouted. I don't want that kind of strength. I don't want to be dragged into this, and I don't want to drag anyone else down, either. Don't say that. Kojima's voice was calm. We know right from wrong. But we need to see, we need proof that all our pain and suffering will be rewarded. I told you this isn't just about us anymore. That's why your eye is the way it is, and why I have my signs. That's why we met. Events always have meaning, Kojima said. There's meaning in overcoming pain and suffering. That's right, Momose said in a deep voice, and you've got to drag everybody into it. I flashed a look at Kojima. It was her face, but Momose's voice. Then when I thought I heard Kojima's voice again, it was Momose's face. We're not talking about some fantasy, she said, we're talking about reality. You don't need imagination, you don't need anything. It's just the obvious truth. Laughter split the air. I couldn't figure out whose voice it was. Momose's? Their voices hummed together, and their faces mixed so that I couldn't tell them apart. I closed my eyes and shook my head.

When I opened my eyes, Kojima was still laughing.

Ninomiya had his eyes locked on Kojima. He wasn't saying anything. Kojima stroked his cheek with her right hand. I could tell from where I stood how tense he was. Kojima smiled and lifted her hand to pet him on the head. He made a face I'd never seen him make before. He was blushing, cheeks splotchy red. He was clenching his fists, unable to move. When she was done with Ninomiya, Kojima walked toward Momose. She moved as if sleepwalking, but every step was firm.

When Kojima reached out to touch Momose, Ninomiya came to his senses and ran over to tackle her. He grabbed her hair from behind and threw her down into a puddle. I could hear marbles of water beating down on her back. I dropped the rock and tumbled toward her. Ninomiya looked down at the two of us. His face was bright red. Momose uncrossed his arms and touched his lips. The half-moons of his eyes were fixed upon Kojima. He looked pleased.

"Hey! What are you doing?"

Someone was yelling at us from outside the park. I spun around. A middle-aged woman holding an umbrella in one hand and a couple of plastic shopping bags in the other was peering into the park, watching us. Ninomiya gave Momose a quick slap on the arm before running off. Momose ran in the other direction.

The woman came toward us.

"What the hell is going on?"

Kojima was naked on her back, still laughing but otherwise motionless. I sat her up, then picked up each piece of clothing she had taken off and draped it, soaking, over her. As the rain grew weaker, the sun became stronger. Kojima's skin glistened white in the sunlight. She leaned against me and laughed through her tears. Thick tears dripping from her eyes mixed with the mud and rain all over her face. "I know it hurt," I said. "Kojima! I know it hurt! I know it hurt!" It was all I could say. I was crying my eyes out too.

"Hey, where are your clothes?" the woman asked. "You two, where are your clothes?" Her shopping bags squeaked against each other.

"Stay here," the woman said and shook my shoulder.

But I didn't react. I just called Kojima's name, over and over, rubbing her back. She didn't answer me. She was still crying, still laughing. I leaned in and held her head in my arms. I couldn't stop crying. My tears fell on Kojima's face, mixing with her tears and the rain. But I wasn't crying because I was sad. I guess I was crying because we had nowhere else to go, no choice but to go on living in this world. Crying because we had no other world to choose, and crying at everything before us, everything around us. I kept calling Kojima's name. After a while, more adults arrived. Kojima kept her eyes on me until they wrapped her in a blanket and carried her away. That was the last time I saw her.

I never had another friend like her. She was the only one.

CHAPTER NINE

Mom and I sat across from each other at the kitchen table, the way we did at dinner. Neither of us said anything. She made me tea, then got up again to pour some for herself, as if it were an afterthought. When she saw that my cup was empty, she got up to make another pot. We went through this over and over.

Two days had passed since what happened at Whale Park.

I hadn't gone back to school. Teachers and parents came to our house in droves, but Mom wouldn't let them in. She sent them away, telling them that she would go to the school to say what she had to say. I stayed in my room.

"It's like on TV," she said, "when a kid won't come out of their room, and the mom leaves their dinner on a tray right outside the door. If they're studying for exams, she'll bring the tray all the way in, but otherwise she leaves it outside, right? Then she comes back later on, the plate's clean, and she carries everything back into the kitchen. You know what I mean? This was my first time doing that." She laughed uneasily. "How can I say it . . ."

"What?" I asked.

"Well, I'm glad I could do that for you."

"Oh."

"I need to stop by the school, but I wanted to talk to you about something first."

"Okay."

"When these things happen, people like to gossip."

"I know."

"But you're the only one I'm listening to."

"I know."

"You can say anything. Or nothing, if that's what you want to do."

I told her about being bullied.

About the past year, and everything before that. I thought that it would take all day, but when I started talking, it took no time at all. Once I had put my thoughts and feelings into words, it felt like it had only lasted a few minutes. Mom rested her cheek on her palm, nodding now and then, listening to everything I had to say.

"The way I see it," she said, after a long pause, turning her teacup in her hands, "you don't have to go to school. But high school won't be like this. If you want to keep going to school, we can find a way to make that happen."

"Okay."

"But no one's going to make you go," she said. "You don't have to."

"Okay."

"We'll make it work. Whatever you want to do." She smiled. "Let's just talk about it."

Then I told her about my eyes. About not knowing what to do. About how I had no way of knowing if the surgery would work, but wondered if even considering it meant I was giving up. I told her about Kojima and how she told me that my eyes were who I was, and that without my eyes I wouldn't be myself, and how much that meant to me, how special it was. I took my time. Mom just listened. And even though I wasn't sure I should, I told her about my real mom. About how she had had a lazy eye, too. I had this photograph of her where I could see it.

*

Mom listened, gazing at her fingers, lined up on the table. She took her cup and got up for more tea. I heard water filling the kettle, then the stove clicking on. After a while, the water started to boil. We listened to it for a really long time, as if that sound meant something to us.

"I don't think I ever told you this, but I knew her, your real mom," she said.

"You were friends?" I asked.

"Not exactly, but I knew her," she said from the kitchen. "I wasn't sure you even remembered what she looked like, but I figured that you knew her eyes were like yours, from a photo or something. That's why when you brought it up before, your eyes, I didn't know how to react. I knew you probably associated it with your mom, and that it wasn't really my place to say anything. More than that, it just always seemed natural to me. There's nothing wrong with having a lazy eye."

Mom and I were quiet for a minute.

"Know what?" she said, looking at me. "I think you should have it done."

I looked at her.

"It's up to you, of course. But I still think you should do it. Eyes are just eyes. You won't lose anything. What stays will stay, and what won't, won't."

"Yeah."

"Would you have to stay in the hospital?" she asked, taking a seat.

"They said that, at my age, it would be one night, at most."

"What, that's it?" she laughed. "It feels like it should be a bigger deal than that. More dramatic."

"Yeah, maybe," I laughed. Mom laughed too.

"Well, don't worry about the cost," she said, with an air of finality. "If you're going to do it, you should have the best doctor in the country."

"The doctor said that young doctors do this procedure all the time," I said.

"Seriously?"

"He said basically anyone can do it."

"But that's got nothing to do with the cost, right?" she frowned. "This is eye surgery we're talking about. It's got to be pretty expensive."

"He said it costs 15,000 yen."

"That's all?" Mom asked. "15,000?"

"There he is!"

When he saw me, the doctor held his hand up near his face and grinned. Mom and I bowed in response. It was a sunny afternoon. The lobby was crowded as always, tinged with that smell you only find in hospitals. Mom bowed again. She thanked the doctor for fitting us into his busy schedule and began asking about the procedure. I whispered to her that he wasn't the one doing the surgery.

"Oh," she said, embarrassed, and bowed again, this time in apology. The doctor laughed and told her not to worry.

"He's a good friend. A good doctor, too. Believe it or not, strabismus happens to be his area of expertise. Plenty of patients come here just to see him."

"Thank you so much for introducing us." Mom bowed again.

The doctor laughed, assuring her it wasn't any trouble.

"It's good to have this done while you're still young. No time like the present."

He smiled, and we nodded, taking his word for it.

They made small talk for a minute. A nurse on the loudspeaker was calling someone's name over and over. Orderlies stood by, chatting. Nurses led old people past us, taking careful steps. We watched the scene, but my head was somewhere else. After a while, they called my name. Mom went over to the reception desk to fill out my intake form and whatever paper-work they needed for the surgery.

"Take a quick walk?" the doctor asked me.

I told Mom we'd be right outside.

"Do you have other patients you need to see?" I asked the doctor as we walked.

"Not on Wednesday afternoons," he said, staving off a yawn. He stretched like he was just waking up. "Did you go with the local anesthetic?"

"No, general."

"Are you scared?" he smiled.

"Just a little," I laughed.

"Yeah, I can't blame you," he said, and really yawned this time. "It's warm out, especially considering how cold it's been this week."

It was a bright December day. An easy day, when all the minutes fit together. We sat down on a bench and people-watched. There were all kinds of noises. Bicycle bells ringing. Kids crying. A jackhammer in the distance. Closer to us, there were birds chirping. The wind wasn't strong, but it was constant. Its sound filled everything around us, nestling among the trees.

"I don't even know why I'm here," I heard myself say. It felt like the words had hopped out of my mouth. "I don't know if it's right."

"That's okay," the doctor said. Then we just sat there.

"Why am I doing this?" I said like I was talking to myself.

"You have a lazy eye. Do you need any other reason?"

I was quiet.

"People are always changing. Just look at your nose. Remember how swollen it was? Now it's as good as new. This surgery isn't any different. Know what I mean?"

The doctor leaned back into the bench and stretched his hands over his head, rolling his neck in circles.

"You're so young. You have your whole life ahead of you.

If the surgery's successful, you'll adjust to your new eyes in no time. Before long," he laughed, "you won't even remember what it was like."

"Think so?" I asked. "You think I'll really forget?"

"I know so," he said. "You won't even remember that you can't remember. Unlike some people."

Then he tapped his nose with his forefinger and started cracking up.

"Chopstick."

We both laughed.

I smelled disinfectant and recognized the white sheets of the hospital bed. Feeling was returning to my hands and feet. The surgery was over and the anesthetic was wearing off. A voice asked how I felt, and I turned to see my mom. She looked concerned. I touched my face and found a mass of gauze over my right eye, but I could feel my eyeball roll around under the layers. It felt a little sore, but not anything I would describe as painful.

"You'll stay here tonight. I'll take you home in the morning," Mom said. "Okay?" My head was still foggy. I tried to nod without sitting up.

A little bit later, the ophthalmologist came by to ask if I was in pain. I told him I felt fine. He pressed his thumb onto the bandage over my eye, then told me about what to expect going forward. He said the surgery was a success, then told me how often to use the eyedrops and when I was supposed to start physical therapy. He explained that it would take some time before my eye muscles developed and that I'd need to schedule regular checkups. I nodded vaguely. Before I knew it, I was fast asleep.

The next day, Mom came to the hospital at lunch to pick me up. I waited for her to complete the discharge forms, and then we left. It was bright out, the blue sky stretching cloudlessly in every direction. I thought I would be fine with just my left eye, since that was all that I had ever had, but I was having trouble walking. It was probably the bandage. Mom and I didn't talk at all. Partway home, she realized she had left her insurance card at the hospital and said to wait there while she went back to get it.

I was standing in the middle of the tree-lined street.

With both eyes closed, I peeled the bandage from my right eye, put on my glasses, and opened my eyes, slowly.

The scene before me was one I'd never even dreamed of.

In the cold December air, all the leaves, thousands upon thousands of them, flashed against the sky, drenched in gold. Every leaf rang with its own light, and all the light poured into me without end. I inhaled and surrendered to the flow. The distance between one second and the next felt stretched out by the hands of some enormous being. I forgot to breathe, forgot to blink, and I let myself sink into the fragrant black bark of the trees. I could feel their skin against the softest parts of my body. With the tips of my fingers, I caught the drops of light falling through the gaps in the humming leaves and even entered them. It was noon, but the sun was out of sight. Everything glowed on its own. My mouth agape, I shook my head, unable to admit that this scenery was real. I bent down to pick up a leaf and examine it. It had a weight that I had never felt, a coolness that I had never known, a definite shape. The tears spilled from my eyes, and the world before me, appearing through a blur of tears, continuously split apart and hatched anew.

Everything was beautiful. At the end of the street, a street I had walked down more times than I could count, I saw the other side for the first time, glowing white. I understood it. Through my tears, I saw the world come into focus. The world had depth now. It had another side. I opened my eyes as wide as I could, fighting to see it all. Everything that I could see was beautiful. I cried and cried, standing there, surrounded by that beauty, even though I wasn't standing anywhere. I could hear the sound of my own tears. Everything was beautiful. Not that there was anyone to share it with, anyone to tell. Just the beauty.